ROBERT FROST

Robert Frost with his schnauzers
at the Homer Noble farmhouse
Ripton, Vermont c. 1960-61

ROBERT FROST

Contours of Belief

Dorothy Judd Hall

Ohio University Press
Athens, Ohio
London

Library of Congress Cataloging in Publication Data

Hall, Dorothy Judd.
   Robert Frost : contours of belief.

   Bibliography: p.
   Includes index.
   1. Frost, Robert, 1874-1963—Religion and ethics. 2. Religion in literature. I. Title.
PS3511.R94Z74   1983   811'.52   83-4247
ISBN 0-8214-0672-8

To Lesley
my dear and longtime friend
for being the one above all
who believed this book into being
and
to my husband Bill
for his loving and persistent help
at every stage of the writing

Contents

On Authenticity viii

Acknowledgments ix

In Memoriam x

Introduction by Lesley Frost xi

Preface xv

I AFTERIMAGES 1

II TRUSTING IN CONTRARIES 13

III GRACE NOTES 26

IV A MERCY-JUSTICE CROSS 36

V AN ACCEPTABLE SACRIFICE 48

VI THE HOLINESS OF WHOLENESS 60

VII ALL REVELATION 72

VIII AN ANNUNCIATION 86

IX SALVATION IN SURRENDER 100

X THE TRIAL BY EXISTENCE 114

Endnotes 125

Selected Bibliography 135

Index 144

On Authenticity

In most respects, quotations from Frost's poetry conform to the 1949 edition of *Complete Poems of Robert Frost* and the 1962 edition of *In the Clearing*. My decision not to use the more recent (1969) complete-in-one-volume *The Poetry of Robert Frost*, edited by Edward Connery Lathem, was based mainly on information in an essay by Donald Hall (no relation to me), "Robert Frost Corrupted," dated 1982 and printed in his *The Weather for Poetry*. He states that Lathem makes "1,364 emendations, of which his notes justify 247 by reference to earlier printings. Thus he makes 1,117 changes for which he offers no textual sources . . ."

Most emendations involve only punctuation, but, as Hall points out, even these changes can affect rhythm and meaning. I find Lathem's unexplained substitution of *take* for *choose* in the title and text of "Choose Something Like a Star" particularly puzzling, since I recall hearing Frost say *choose* whenever he recited the poem at Bread Loaf, Vermont, in the summers just before his death. (He always carried a copy of the *Complete Poems* to his readings.) In fact, the question of *choice*—of human free will—is a dominant concern in his poetry.

I have, then, adhered to the two earlier volumes, except for using, like Lathem, double quotation marks where *Complete Poems* uses single, and Roman characters for the tercet on page 74, which is italicized in *In The Clearing*. Two poems quoted do not appear in any of the above collections: "Parting" comes from Lawrance Thompson's *Robert Frost: The Early Years*; the untitled poem beginning "To prayer I think I go" comes from Untermeyer's *The Letters of Robert Frost to Louis Untermeyer*.

DJH

Acknowledgments

For the helpful discussions and kind encouragement they provided over many years I thank Emily K. Dalgarno and John Malcom Brinnin, who directed the doctoral dissertation behind this book; Rabbi Victor E. Reichert and his wife Louise, whose friendship with Robert Frost brought me closer in spirit to the poet himself; Father Arthur MacGillivray and William Alfred, whose anecdotal memories of the poet come to life in these pages; Gerald Fitzgerald, whose intimate knowledge of the sonnet form alerted me to subtle nuances in "Design"; and long before them all, Robert L. Lowe, who so sensitively guided my master's thesis on Frost's "lyric voice." I pay tribute to the memory of Lawrance Thompson for his generous expression of concern with my project, in a long letter (1970) where he anticipated complexities I must deal with and even envisioned the theological categories that "would" organize this study. I thank my father and my many friends for sharing with me the joy of this accomplishment. Finally, I am especially grateful to Bill, my husband, for his handsome line drawings and book jacket and to Lesley Frost for her glowing introduction. I offer a poetic "grace note" by Lesley—she wrote it out for me on a visit to Boston nearly twenty years ago. It surely partakes of her father's emblematic spiritual vision:

SYMBOLISM

These hieroglyphs of snow
In wheelrut pond and ditch,
The tracks of quail and doe
Like quilting overstitch,
Can only just imply
The truth of what they say:
That bird and beast passed by
And winter came this way.

In Memoriam

As the page proofs for this book were being completed, Lesley Frost died in Fairfield, Connecticut (July 1983). She was my close friend, and I had hoped to deliver her copy of the book, whose contents she knew so well, myself. Throughout her life she worked tirelessly to help keep her father's memory vital and to pursue her own writing, teaching, speaking, and other projects, for which we will long remember her.

DJH

A slightly different version of Lesley's "Introduction" appeared in *Frost: Centennial Essays* III—ed. Jac Tharpe: University Press of Mississippi, 1978—under the title "In Aladdin's Lamp Light." When Dr. Tharpe asked Lesley for an article, she suggested the "Introduction" (which she had already written for me), and it was published with the understanding that it would eventually appear here.

DJH

Introduction
by LESLEY FROST

A question being asked of late, did Robert Frost have any defined belief in an Almighty, is now being bravely considered in *Robert Frost: Contours of Belief*, by Dorothy Judd Hall. Naturally, there have been countless references—articles, essays, sermons—to the *religion* in my father's poetry. There are two notable studies of the poem "Directive": one, " 'Directive' and the Spiritual Journey," by Robert K. Greenleaf; another, "A Reading of Robert Frost's 'Directive,' " by John Robert Doyle. There is the fine biography by Elizabeth Sergeant, *Robert Frost: The Trial by Existence*, using the poem of that name for its title; there are sermons by Rabbi Victor Reichert; Elizabeth Isaacs' *Introduction to Robert Frost*; and the many publications, in our academic journals, of articles by Dorothy Hall herself, as she made this book an important goal. Often, too, the subject has been raised in an interview with my father, such as one he gave to Selden Rodman (*Tongues of Fallen Angels*) in the Bread Loaf days. They are discussing a Frost poem "The Bear," and Rodman asks if it isn't meant to be "a sly criticism of preachers." Frost replies, "Could *be*. I despise religiosity. But I have no religious doubts. Not about God's existence, anyway."

Dorothy Hall has so ably stated the case in the affirmative, in God's favor, and I find it so easy to agree with her, that I am wondering how we all became involved with the question in the beginning. However, it had its roots long before my time. As a boy, Robert was steeped in the religion of a mother to whom he was strongly attached: a gallant, intelligent woman of Scotch descent, with poetic leanings of her own. Isabel (Belle) Moodie Frost was a devout Swedenborgian, as her Church in San Francisco can testify, and she was with her son during his adolescence and youth. When his father died and they returned East, she founded a private grade school in which he was a pupil. He lived at home while he attended the Lawrence High School (where he was a classmate of Elinor White—a case in point for love at sight— "Meeting and Passing," "The Telephone"). After a few months at Dartmouth he returned home to assist his mother in the school. Three years later he married Elinor, and together they taught there.

Thus the direct influence of Belle Moodie Frost on Robert should not be underestimated. The reason my father claimed he read his first *book* when he was fourteen (one of his slight exaggerations) was that he had been read-aloud-to over those years from the books *she* chose: Scotland's history, Robert Burns' poems (that were to give me my name—Lesley). *Tales of a Grandfather* (Sir Walter Scott), the teachings of Swedenborg, MacDonald's *At the Back of The North Wind*, Prescott's *Conquest of Peru* and *Conquest of Mexico*. (My father's first poem, "La Noche Triste"—written when he was sixteen—was a ballad of Cortez in Mexico City.)

True, now that my attention has been called to it, I find it interesting to mark a certain growth of his religious position from, shall we say, "A Prayer in Spring" to "A Steeple on the House" and "Directive." In 1962, or thereabouts, he remarked to me, "I have always lived according to my emotions, perhaps too much so, but I wouldn't have had it otherwise." Comes the question, what did he mean by emotions. I expect for him they were the "passionate preference[s] such as love at sight" ("Accidentally on Purpose"). Love was the original source, an instinctual way, through nature, of being in touch with Divinity. Perhaps love *was* Divinity.

But from there on he began to seek a Somebody who got this all rolling. He needed that Somebody to "speak and tell us where" He is ("Revelation"). The question of salvation came up. Was he one of those to be saved? The answer was drawn for him in the poem "Directive." The orders for how to be saved were clear enough; just follow them religiously. Indeed, one could be so familiar with the Deity as to risk a little sacrilegious banter—a play on both their houses. And so we have "I turned to speak to God . . . " and "Forgive, O Lord . . . "; and the extraordinary *Masque of Reason*, a conversation among God, Job, and the Devil (and Job's wife, don't forget), when God at last explains the purpose of his testing Job's ability to take punishment without protest. It was, He said, His way of "showing off to the Devil" that God's followers were loyal however unjustifiable it all appeared to be. It makes for the best of reasoning by Robert Frost, and who can say—it could be true!

Dorothy Hall carries Frost's sense of the Above and Beyond into many aspects of philosophy and religion including Swedenborg, Emerson, Bergson, William James. Writing on Frost for many years has brought Dorothy an appreciation of the religious motives behind so much of the poetry. As for me, I can only support her verdict by saying that the question, however put, had been unconsciously answered for me in those faraway evenings of being read-aloud-to (an inherited custom) on the Derry Farm in front of the wood fire in the Franklin stove, by the light of an Aladdin lamp. And speaking of wishes, didn't my father also say that wishes wished hard enough would bring them to pass—would be a way of projecting the future? (So he wrote "The Trial by Existence" and "Two Tramps in Mud Time"—"For Heaven and the future's sakes.") There were passages from various hymns, from the Old and New Testaments, *Pilgrim's Progress*, Maeterlinck's *Blue Bird*, Gayley's *Classic Myths*, the *Odyssey*, the *Aeneid, Marco Polo*, "The Ancient Mariner," "Horatius at the Bridge," Tennyson's Arthurian legends, Shakespeare—poetry and more poetry (with a lot of memorizing)—poetry and prose in which the heroic and the Divine rubbed shoulders with the not so heroic and not so Divine, for, as my father insisted, one age is like another, for better or worse, in how it takes to Good and Evil. In other words, there had to be bad for there to be good.

Yes, such poems as "The Trial by Existence" and "Two Tramps in Mud Time," with many others, charted a life course for Robert Frost. "I Could Give All to Time" and "Directive" added the strength needed to run that course and cross the finish line. Since he hasn't returned, nor has anyone, we may assume ("Away!") that he approved of what he found.

Lesley Frost

Lesley Frost   New York City

Preface

I don't go to church, but
I look in the window.

—RF, MIDDLEBURY,
21 MAY 1943
(REGINALD L. COOK,
The Dimensions of
Robert Frost, p. 149.)

Philosophical uncertainty, religious doubt, and even nihilism pervade much twentieth-century literature. A hundred years from now critics will very likely give our age a convenient label, analogous to the "classical," "metaphysical," "romantic" categories of the past. Then again, perhaps they won't quite be able to identify in a word the essence of what we in our nearsightedness call "modern"—and, still more hopelessly disoriented, "postmodern." But whatever name they may devise will have to account for the spiritual unrest at the heart of our writing. Frequently ironic in tone, authors tend to be ambiguous and paradoxical. Styles vary, but they seem to share a common sense of the elusiveness of "Truth." Faulkner's sentences circle endlessly around their meaning like a bird that can never quite capture its prey. Beckett's language lapses almost into silence, as if words, like life itself, may linger only a moment astride the grave of the ineffable. We become spellbound by images of desolation, decadence, and spiritual isolation. T. S. Eliot's "waste land," Fitzgerald's "valley of ashes," Hemingway's "clean, well-lighted place" (set against the brooding night outside) come easily to mind. W. H. Auden called our time an "age of anxiety," and that tag may stick.

Was Robert Frost infected with this disease of anxiety? At one point he offers a diagnosis of our malady: "Space ails us moderns: we are sick with space"—"We're either nothing or a God's regret." And he prescribes a dubious cure: "The groundwork of all faith is human woe" ("The Lesson for Today"). Yet these lines do not reach to the center of Frost's spirituality.

Surer indicators of his belief, or lack of it, are the recurrent dark/light figures in the poetry, with implied shuttling between obscuration and clarity. A naive reader may overlook the strain of darkness—of "terror" often—that Lionel Trilling unmasked in 1959 at the poet's eighty-fifth birthday party; but the more astute had already noticed it.[1] Back in 1934 J. McBride Dabbs observed the frequency of "dark woods" in Frost's rural landscapes and speculated about psychological shadings.[2] Understandably, Dabbs did not carry his inquiry into the realm of religious doubt; psychological or spiritual darkness is not incompatible with faith. A dark-night-of-the-soul may certainly foreshadow conversion. In T. S. Eliot it apparently did. While Frost was "acquainted with the night"—aware of the moral confusion of our age, a "time . . . neither wrong nor right"—he did not undergo any orthodox religious conversion, a point which will reappear in my final chapter. As to the "space-sickness" metaphor, I believe his inner darkness "stretched away unto the edge of doom" like those dark trees of his early poem "Into My Own."

Yet there is light; there is clarification—from the "pasture spring" in *North of Boston* where he went "to watch the water clear," to the "cabin in the clearing" of his last book, with the woods precariously cut back around it. It was the clarification of metaphor. A hard-won enlightenment, for Frost—like his intellectual forebears, the Puritans—used metaphor non-aesthetically. His images spring from the stuff of living, from "leaning . . . hard" on the earth and wresting meaning from experience ("To Earthward"). Moreover, after many years of study I am convinced that this act of *converting* experience into poetry was for him essentially religious. The transformation of life into metaphoric language—the realization of his poetic spirit in verbal material—was the only true spiritual conversion he was concerned with. To commit his vital insights to poetry was for him an act of belief.

"A poem," he tells us in "The Figure a Poem Makes," "ends in a clarification of life—not necessarily a great clarification, such as sects and cults are founded on, but in a momentary stay against confusion."[3] On the basis of this remark some may conclude that Frost turned to poetry as a *substitute* for religious belief, insofar as it satisfied the psychological need to make sense of the world, to bring order out of chaos. I disagree. I offer—especially in my discussion of "Directive"—an alternative to this argument. Others may complain that a mere *momentary* stay is too tentative and betrays a lack of spiritual commitment. The term "spiritual drifter" has often been associated with Frost, since Yvor Winters coined it in 1948.[4] Twelve years later George W. Nitchie explored the "drifting" problem at greater length, and in the more technical language of "teleological uncertainty," "ontological indecisiveness."[5]

Winters' label for Frost caught on, it seems, in the minds of college professors and literary scholars and over the decades became a catch-all for the unspecified feeling among some of them that the poet was an agnostic. About ten years ago when I told a colleague that I was doing research on Frost's religious belief, he replied without hesitation—and with a degree of condescension— "Oh, does he have one?" "Yes," I said, "but I can't quite say what it is." My response pretty much pinpoints the predicament I find myself in: my attempt to "rescue" the poet from Winters' camp-followers should not, as a result, deliver him over to any particular band of "believers"—even those, like the Unitarians, who wish to hold him in a bondage so light that he might not seem to be ensnared at all. As a matter of fact, Frost has been known to take a rather dim view of Unitarianism. Peter J. Stanlis recalls his remark that the "theists" among Unitarians "start with God and believe that God is too good to damn any man and that therefore all men will be saved. Salvation is universal." On the other hand, the "humanitarians" among them "start with man and believe that men are too good to be damned by any God, *if* He exists. So they also end up believing in universal salvation, but in a secular rather than a religious sense."[6] We may remember that Frost also takes a sly swipe at Unitarianism in *A Masque of Mercy*: the evangelistic Paul calls the skeptical Keeper "the kind of Unitarian/Who having by elimination got/From many gods to Three and Three to One,

/Thinks why not taper off to none at all,/Except as father putative to sort of/Legitimize the brotherhood of man." The Thomism in the masque may have encouraged a suspicion that Frost was on the edge of converting to Roman Catholicism, that he was about to take the ontological leap of faith which Jonah started, then failed, to take, with the door to salvation slamming in his face, leaving him to die on the threshold.[7] The masque was published in 1947; as we know, Frost lived another sixteen years and no conversion took place.

So the troublesome question of his religious belief persists. In fairness, we might ask whether belief or disbelief wasn't his own private business. Or, more peevishly, we might throw up our hands and declare, "If it's such a secret, let him *keep* it! What's it got to do with the poetry anyway?" Yet to me it is *integrally* bound up with the poetry. I agree with Frost's official biographer Lawrance Thompson in a letter (22 September 1970) he wrote me a few years before his death:

> I really think that Frost's religious belief provides more problems than any other part of his art—and it happens to be inseparable from his art.

The "God Question"—as Frost himself called it—cannot, then, be set aside in considering his work, notwithstanding the difficulties involved in posing it, let alone answering it. An independent Yankee, he eschewed both orthodox theology and doctrinaire thinking. But he was deeply religious. How can we sound him out spiritually without reducing his belief to abstract formulae? His essay "The Constant Symbol" proclaims in a mock-liturgical tone, "The bard has said in effect, Unto these forms did I commend the spirit."[8] I think the directive is clear: we must search for his belief in his poetic metaphors. The search is not an easy one, for Frost deliberately sets up verbal and stylistic barriers to over-facile thinking. In the end, an *approximation* of his belief may be all we can hope to attain. But, as he tells us in "Education by Poetry," "everything depends on the closeness with which you come, and you ought to be marked for the closeness, for nothing else."[9] "Progress," he says, "is not the aim, but circulation. The thing is to get

among the poems where they hold each other apart in their places
as the stars do" ("The Prerequisites").[10] Thus I have chosen to cir-
culate thematically among the poems, juxtaposing the earlier with
the later, rather than to "progress" chronologically. I have found a
great deal of consistency in his thinking, complex though it is.
There is an overriding consciousness of design in his poetry that
is apparently a synecdochic expression of his faith in the possibility of universal form and meaning. It links the artist in him to what
he intuitively perceives as a comprehensive, if sometimes incon-
gruous, cosmic structure.

We find this sense of design, for example, in the way a later
poem, "All Revelation," harkens back in title and theme to the
early and simpler "Revelation," as each clarifies the other. Also, it
seems only partly accidental that the prophetic movement into
the "vastness" of "dark trees" ("Into My Own") at the outset of his
first volume finds its fulfillment in the untitled final poem of his
last. There he turns from the *momentary* sanctuary of the metaphoric clearing that gives the book its name, and sets forth into
unknown regions—moving "against the trees" and leaving behind
him "shadowy tracks/Across the tinted snow." According to his
daughter Lesley, he delayed sending *In the Clearing* to the print-
er, having a premonition that he must write one more poem to
conclude it.

I have taken the clue for my circulatory method—and for my
book title—from a piece of advice Frost offered a reporter in
1955. I think it bears repeating:

> If you would learn the way a man feels about God, don't ask him to
> put a name on himself. All that is said with names is soon not
> enough.

> If you would have out the way a man feels about God, watch his
> life, hear his words. Place a coin, with its denomination unknown,
> under paper and you can tell its mark by rubbing a pencil over the
> paper. From all the individual rises and valleys your answer will
> come out.[11]

The metaphor is convincing. Like a coin under a sheet of paper,
Frost's religious "denomination" is hidden, cannot be named. But

in "rubbing" the verbal and metaphoric surfaces of his poetry, we "can tell" the *contours of his belief.*

Let's not forget, though, that every coin has two sides, and I'm aware of the contours on the flip-side in Frost's case. His poetic landscapes are etched with grim pictures of physical degeneration, perhaps most powerfully in the "universal cataract of death" of "West-Running Brook." His constellating stars give the illusion of an intrinsic pattern but are morally neutral, blank as some "Minerva's snow-white marble eyes/Without the gift of sight" ("Stars"). His "desert places" overwhelm with celestial and psychic emptiness. We must look to Sartre's *Nausea* to find an emptiness as total—in Roquentin's more earthbound anti-vision of pure meaningless existence, emerging from the roots of a chestnut tree. Out of a sinister drama in the world of flowers, insects, and arachnids, Frost deliberately constructs a questionable argument for order—and gives it the ironic title "Design." The skillful rhetoric of its lines, filled with "characters of death and blight," barely avoids yielding to the dark alternatives of a governing malevolence or pervasive chaos. In "The Draft Horse" he presents similar forbidding options, moving into the very heart of darkness "with a lantern that wouldn't burn." Not always so fraught with terror, his *clearings* are nevertheless ringed by metaphysical obscurity, "by a world of doubt surrounded" ("Beech").

Returning to the figure of the coin, we might wonder which side is *heads*, which *tails*? Which carries the "mark"? A reader evaluating this study for my publisher takes an imaginative look at the question:

> I am reminded of the mirrored universes of science fiction, of matter/anti-matter fantasies, as I see shadowed behind Hall's contour, the contour of "disbelief."

The analogy between Frost's mirror images and inversions in the realm of physics is a new, inventive way of perceiving an old literary paradox: the coexistence in Frost of seemingly contradictory religious attitudes. In 1941—some years before Yvor Winters called Frost a "spiritual drifter"—Hyatt Howe Waggoner decided that the poet was "an agnostic in respect to the orthodox Christian creeds."[12] Waggoner was apparently seeking to align Frost with some recognizable branch of Christianity. His failure to find substantial parallels was, I think, due to his turning to the *New* Testament for a clue to Frost's lack of orthodoxy. As a matter of fact, the poet called himself "an *Old* Testament Christian," a designation that further obstructs any attempt to pin down the nature of his *un*orthodoxy.[13] Waggoner, not altogether satisfied with his own use of *agnostic*, speculates that Frost "nevertheless knows that life could not have come out of the universe had the germ of life not been instinct in the universe itself." This comment smacks of vitalism and does contain a measure of accuracy, for Henri Bergson's idea of an *élan vital* is discernable in certain poems—particularly in "West-Running Brook" and "Kitty Hawk."[14] Waggoner's early stumbling shows how effective were the trip-wires and pitfalls which Frost carefully left behind himself to slow up eager readers, bent on overtaking him with some ready-to-fit category—or bent, at least, on understanding what categories would *not* fit!

Lawrance Thompson, in an early work on Frost's poetry—*Fire and Ice* (1942)—devotes an entire chapter to assessing the "opposed viewpoints" of "religious faith" and "religious agnosticism" in poems that "may help to explain each other" but "may also contradict each other." Thompson is careful to distinguish between contradictory postures struck in individual poems and "the course of [Frost's] nonaesthetic, or moral, life."[15] He finds "moderation" to be the key to Frost's moral position: "skepticism acts as a balance wheel which controls the accelerations of faith and the decelerations of denial."[16] He is correct, I think, in making a distinction between Frost's life and his art, but I do not feel that skepticism can equalize, or "balance," faith and denial. Rather, it *cancels* faith.

While in Thompson's hands Frost's skeptical tendencies become virtues, other critics have been inclined either, like Yvor Winters, to disparage them or, more sympathetically, to justify them. For example, in 1953 Joseph Warren Beach termed Frost a skeptic, but qualified the judgment by ascribing to him "a very firm set . . . of tastes, of preferences, of values to which he is loyal."[17] Three years later Beach explored the problem further, finding Frost "a refined modern agnostic" who "has retained the aura of New England transcendentalism without a trace of its philosophy."[18]

Beach's "tastes," "preferences," and "aura" seem painfully vague for a scholar of his stature and confirm the perplexing nature of Frost's inconsistencies. The "God Question" has no ultimate resolution, just interpretations to be offered, more or less viable. For some time now, the contour-sleuths have been busy with speculations about Frost's "disbelief." It's time to turn the coin over.

The "Question" is complicated by a measure of prudentiality in Frost. Once after reading aloud "Provide, Provide," the poem about "the withered hag" who has fallen from Hollywood stardom, he warned bitterly, "Or somebody's going to provide *for* you!" In other words: look out for yourself, or someone will deal with you in his *own* self-interest. The prize-winning pullet in "A Blue Ribbon at Amesbury" knows instinctively how to take care of *her*self. Like its companion "A Drumlin Woodchuck," that poem is an Aesop-like fable about a prudent little animal. The fine plumage of this "almost perfect bird" may fade in time, but she will not abdicate her station of eminence on the perch with the "common . . . flock." Her renown may pass, but the hencoop is her bastion:

> The lowly pen is yet a hold
> Against the dark and wind and cold
> To give a prospect to a plan
> And warrant prudence in a man.

The *double entendre* is evident; the "lowly pen" can prove mightier than the sword for any crafty poet whose metaphoric structures act as barrier to cold, shifting philosophical winds, as shield against the darkness of disbelief. Are we to infer that Frost's poems are merely *prudential artistic* arrangements? If so, they would have little bearing on the question of religion—except, as I suggested earlier, to serve as palliative for the loss of it, a *quid-pro-quo* response to the human "rage for order" (to adopt Wallace Stevens' phrase and point of view). Belief and poetry would then display an inverse relationship: as the gods depart, art fills the gap. If in each "momentary stay against confusion" Frost sought only a *psychological* zone of safety from a "background . . . shading away . . . into black and utter chaos,"[19] his poetry would not partake of spiritual illumination. But the clarifications he has achieved are intended to "stroke faith the right way."[20] *The New England of Robert Frost*, a documentary film, shows him in his Ripton, Vermont, log cabin, reflecting on his long career: "Writing a poem has always solved something for me. Giving anything form gives you confidence in the universe—that *it* has form." He was attracted by the idea of human collaboration in an incremental cosmic design, and he found a parallel between God and poet as *makers*. The late poem "Kitty Hawk" tells us that "the supreme merit/Lay in risking spirit/In substantiation." This spiritual risk relates human action to the divine. For the poet, *words* are the medium for substantiating—giving concrete form to—the spirit, so that he may "by craft or art/ . . . give the part/Wholeness in a sense." Frost regarded metaphor as a synecdochic mode of making inroads upon a larger design. Each metaphoric fragment, however tiny, bears witness to belief in an overall unity.

The idea of clarification by metaphor underlies the image of "a cabin in the clearing" in the title poem of Frost's last volume. Like a poem, the cabin is of human manufacture, put together by hand. (Recall the admonition in "New Hampshire": "Nothing not built with hands of course is sacred.") In the midst of dark woods, the "sleepers in [the] house" apparently don't "know where they are" and certainly not "who/They are." Their memory store of "accumulated fact" will probably not "of itself take fire" like a pile of oily rags, "and light the world up." But "They've been here long enough/To push the woods back from around the house," and their effort to understand their "plight" has intrinsic value insofar as it is an *intelligent* response: "Putting the lamp out [for the night] has not put their thought out." Their mental lamp may not shine with the brightness of a sun, but it does illumine. The land they have cleared is an objective correlative of the region of inner clarification they seek, and the light of their spirit is undimmed.

A useful contrast to Frost's *cabin* image is Hemingway's Spanish café in the short story "A Clean, Well-Lighted Place." An old waiter in the café, which is closing for the night, has faith—if that's the right word—only in "nada," in nothing. He mutters an ironic prayer: "Our nada who art in nada, nada be thy name thy kingdom nada thy will be nada in nada as it is in nada. . . ." Talking to himself as he switches off the electric bulb, he knows "it was all a nothing and a man was nothing too." For a lingering patron, who is finally turned out into the night, the "well-lighted" café has offered the comfort of human contact, the numbing warmth of brandy, "a certain cleanness and order" in a worn-out life that hasn't much coherence. In effect, the café represents a refuge from the pain of loneliness, the incompleteness of living. There the perplexities of the world are avoided; they are neither resolved nor clarified in an intellectual or spiritual way.

Hemingway's story and Frost's poem—two nocturnal pieces— alike recognize the conflict between man's emotional needs and the indifference of nature. But Hemingway's café is an area of *escape* from the surrounding dark, whereas Frost's clearing is an *infringement* upon it. The inhabitants of the cabin are surely not "nothing"; they are people who make a difference in the world by staking a human claim, a territory. To use the language of "Kitty Hawk," they "Have no hallowing fears/Anything's forbidden/ Just because it's hidden"; they follow the injunction to "Trespass and encroach." The glow of their intellect, even when it has no physical counterpart, is sustained. In the Hemingway story, however, to extinguish the electric light is to yield to darkness and *nada*.

Nada in Hemingway, like *le néant* in Sartre, predicates an existentially "absurd" condition without inherent meaning or moral frame, a situation where the fundamental human directions are withdrawal—even into suicide (the patron in Hemingway's café attempts hanging himself)—or revolt against the irrational. Camus' *Myth of Sisyphus* is a classic treatise on these difficult choices. But the world view implicit in Frost's poetry increases man's alternatives, for a sense of *nothingness*—found in certain poems— does not become the sole determinant of his vision. In "West-Running Brook" the entropic movement of "everything that runs away/ . . . To fill the abyss' void with emptiness" competes with a "backward motion toward the source,/Against the stream"; the descending current is "Flung backward on itself" in a "white wave" that interrupts the downward flow of the "black stream." "As if regret were in it and were sacred," the trend toward dissolution is offset by a tendency toward evolving design, a structuring process in which man plays a major role.

Throughout the poetry, destruction and creativity coexist in rivalry. "Waste," Frost asserts in "Pod of the Milkweed," is "of the essence of the scheme." Yet concealed within all his conflicting opposites may even be a paradoxical principle of complementarity: "some dim secret of the good of waste"—a notion quite likely derived from what he called Emerson's "good of evil born." The poem "Quandary" justifies the presence of "bad" in the name of equilibrium: "There had to be, I understood,/For there to have been any good."

> It was by having been contrasted
> That good and bad so long had lasted.

After reading this couplet at the Bread Loaf (Vermont) Writers' Conference in 1961, he went on, "Then you've got to say: If good owes so much to bad, bad must be good. I have to work that out—I write them in the train." In Frost a blend of Bible, Emerson, and Bergson counteracts Lucretian materialism, deflects existential meaninglessness. "This uncertain age in which we dwell" has no premium on grief, we learn in "The Lesson for Today"; "One age is like another for the soul." Loss and evil, purposeless in man's eyes, are "universals, not confined/To any one time, place, or human kind." Like their opposites, gain and good, they are tightly woven into the fabric of whatever scheme there may be.

In 1935 Frost wrote a "Letter to *The Amherst Student*" where he explicitly describes the imperative under which man lives. "Suggestions of form in the rolling clouds of nature" demand, not merely invite, man's imitation. Frost assigns to the universal potential for form-making a moral dimension: "There is at least so much good in the world that it admits of form and the making of form. And not only admits of it, but calls for it."[21] He interprets this *calling* as a summons from creation itself. It is not unlike a religious vocation (remember the Latin *vocare*, to call). The poet as "maker"—from the Greek *poiētēs*, one who makes—can be thought of as engaged in a "sacred" activity.

A few years later (1939), adopting a theological idiom, Frost reinforced the idea of the religious function of a poem: "The figure a poem makes . . . must be more felt than seen ahead like prophecy. It must be a revelation, or a series of revelations."[22] Chapter VII of this study explores the link Frost perceived between metaphoric and spiritual revelation. The connection depends upon the capacity of the human mind to interact with physical matter (see the poem "All Revelation"), a concept rooted in Emerson's view of the *visible* as "dial-plate of the invisible" and in the Puritan typological tradition. Frost's New England heritage may account for his predisposition to read natural phenomena as spiritual *figurae*, or "types," but he looked through a darker glass and his angle of vision was skewed. From his vantage point he saw and challenged a universe which relinquishes only infrequent hints of the "Secret" that "sits in the middle" ("The Secret Sits"). Nevertheless, his clarifications were intended as insights into the essential meaning of reality, and his legacy of "words that have become deeds"[23] embodies a distinctly religious commitment.

I

Afterimages

Imagery and after-imagery are about all there is to poetry. Synecdoche and synecdoche.—My motto is that something must be left to God.

—RF (SEE J. McBRIDE DABBS,
"ROBERT FROST AND THE DARK WOODS,"
Yale Review, MARCH 1934, 514-515.)

"AFTER APPLE-PICKING"

It is several decades since I first saw Robert Frost at Barnard College in the early fifties, and a number of "afterimages"— mental snapshots I took of him—are stored in my memory. I see him, in February 1960, in his white frame cottage in South Miami, Florida, sitting on a worn sofa, shirt collar unbuttoned, talking about the citrus trees outside in the garden. (His daughter Lesley had placed me strategically on his "good-ear" side.) I see him there, after about half an hour, shuffling over to his wooden writing desk to poke around for a copy of his latest Christmas-card poem, "A-Wishing Well," and inscribing it for me.

I see him on summer evenings high in the Green Mountains of Vermont, at Bread Loaf School of English, "saying" his own poems as the sun, beyond the latticed French doors of the Little Theatre, sank below the ranging hills. Then I hear the tremolo in his voice, the tone of affection that filtered through his readings from *The Oxford Book of Verse*: a Shakespeare sonnet, a lyric by Coventry Patmore or Walter Savage Landor. (He admired Landor's keeping a strong lyric voice into his eighties—and his epigram on Nature and Art: "I warmed both hands before the fire of life,/It sinks, and I am ready to depart.") And I hear him thunder forth the heroic rhythms of mad Kit Smart's "A Song to David."

I see him entrancing large crowds with wit and poetry in New York City, at Hunter College and at the YMHA uptown on Lexington Avenue. Finally, I see him waiting for the down-elevator at the Astor in winter just a year before he died, after the annual banquet of the Poetry Society of America where he had talked and been fêted. He was clutching some pink and white carnations he had saved from the clean-up crew.

But my critical odyssey begins in the Barnard College parlor where I hear his response to one of my classmates who had asked if "After Apple-Picking" is about death; whether the phrase "Toward heaven" has any religious meaning behind it. I remember his reply—it made me lose some sleep that night: "It's just a matter of afterimagery."

In time I came to understand more of what Frost meant by *afterimagery*. Back then, though, for my Barnard friend, he came up with the word simply to fend off her question, to avoid talking about religion. He shifted the focus from the theology to the psychology department. A dictionary definition of the psychological term "afterimage" reads: "an image or sensation that stays or comes back after the external stimulus has been withdrawn." Thus Frost's answer was appropriate. "After Apple-Picking" indeed contains a series of sensory afterimages—visual, olfactory, auditory, kinaesthetic. The apple picker, "drowsing off," relives the physical impressions of his day of labor: the vision of "magnified apples," their fruity "scent," their "rumbling sound" going into "the cellar bin," "the ache" in his "instep arch" which "keeps the pressure of a ladder-round" (the ladder *rung*, that is), the "sway" of the ladder "as the boughs bend."

So Frost had told the truth about the poem. But in retrospect I realize that, like Emily Dickinson, he had a Yankee inclination to "tell all the Truth but tell it slant," as she had once put it. I have a definite sense, now, of the religious dimension in "After Apple-Picking" that its author was reluctant to let surface. I notice the backward glance it casts toward the Garden of Eden where the first apple was picked, dooming Adam's progeny henceforth to bodily labor, fatigue, and mortality. Mythically, the poem is about *fallen* man, "overtired" from a day (a lifetime?) of hard work. Yet the apple-picker, in his weariness, is content with his partial accomplishment, unbothered by "two or three/Apples [he] didn't pick upon some bough"—the human lot, Frost often noted, of "unfinished business."

Frost's choice of language at Barnard gathers further meaning. The term "afterimage" moves out from psychology toward religion, the apparent domain of the original question. Is the poem talking merely about nightly "human sleep," as it suggests, or also about the sleep of death—an "afterimage" of our lifetime?[1] We observe how tentatively the suggestion is made. The poem hints at the idea of a protracted sleep (like the woodchuck's hibernation) and then seems to reject it. The idea of a final sleep is fleeting; it is *all but* negated in the ambiguous closing line of the poem:

> One can see what will trouble
> This sleep of mine, whatever sleep it is.
> Were he not gone,
> The woodchuck could say whether it's like his
> Long sleep, as I describe its coming on,
> Or just some human sleep.

A decade after Frost had sent up his verbal smoke screen at
Barnard, he diverted another question about "After Apple-
Picking"—at Bread Loaf. He said that the metaphor in the poem is
"less from science than mythology," and he went on: "True
knowledge is myth, not science or religion. Eden is just so many
apples." This remark possibly confirms the identity of the apple-
picker as a latter-day Adam. While performing the very chore
which sustains him, he symbolically perpetuates the Genesis legacy of mankind's first act of disobedience. He is tired from physical labor and weary, too, of the burden of original sin.

Frost's remark about "myth" helps to clarify the poem, but
what did he mean by elevating myth to the level of "true knowledge" at the expense of science and religion? Some light may be
shed upon this problem by circulating elsewhere among his
words, in verse and prose. We notice that he often challenges us to
examine our notions about knowledge, to reassess our priorities.
His "Too Anxious for Rivers" asks skeptically:

> how much longer a story has science
> Before she must put out the light on the children
> And tell them the rest of the story is dreaming?

The poem implies that the "light" of science—that is, of empirically based knowledge—is not an eternal flame. In Frost's scale of
values, science is a respectable branch of knowledge, but it is not
the sole proprietor of truth. A related point is made in *A Masque
of Reason*, in a provocative passage where God speaks to Job of
human fickleness:

> My forte is truth,
> Or metaphysics, long the world's reproach
> For standing still in one place true forever;
> While science goes self-superseding on.
> Look at how far we've left the current science
> Of Genesis behind. The wisdom there though,
> Is just as good as when I uttered it.
> Still, novelty has doubtless an attraction.

The passage casts doubt upon the modern tendency to give

scientific knowledge preëminence over religious belief. The phrase "current science/Of Genesis" is particularly arresting. In our sophistication we are not accustomed to think of Biblical myth as *science* (as a way of knowing—from the Latin *scio*, to know), much less as *current* (as viable currency). Here the ongoing *novelty* of science, with its evident progress, is assigned a role subordinate to the perpetual sameness of mythic *wisdom*, which is, to God, the enduring *truth*.

Elsewhere, in his essay "The Constant Symbol," Frost declares that "science," like poetry, "is simply made of metaphor" ("if it will take the soft impeachment from a friend"). Applying this sort of logic to the passage in *A Masque of Reason*, we discover there a juxtaposition of two different breeds of metaphor: the so-called *knowledge of science* and the *wisdom of myth*. Consequently, we may read the passage as an assertion by God of the permanent validity of His metaphor for creation, unchanged by the passing "attraction" of newer metaphoric fads.

The claim in the masque, which dates from 1945, that "[God's] forte is truth" is anticipated in a letter from Frost to Bernard De-Voto in 1938:

> Any decent philosophy and all philosophy has to [be] largely static. Else what would there be to distinguish it from science? It is the same with religion: it must be the same yesterday today and forever. The only part of Genesis that has changed in three thousand years and become ridiculous is the science in it. The religion stands.

Thus a consistent line of reasoning connects the letter with *A Masque of Reason*, both subject to some retrospective clarification by the 1946 essay "The Constant Symbol." The consistency appears shaken, however, by Frost's remark at Bread Loaf in the sixties, equating "true knowledge" with "myth, not science or religion." If we are not to charge him with fuzzy thinking, we must, I propose, assume that when he used the term "religion" at Bread Loaf he was referring to religious *dogma*, which, like scientific thought through the centuries, has undergone shifts of interpretation. But he was granting myth—that is, the *essence* of religious belief—the stature of truth.

Identifying the Genesis myth at the heart of "After Apple-Picking" helps us to recognize the intrinsically religious spirit of the poem, which Frost, back at Barnard, was trying to deny. His reply to the undergraduate was correct, but it was carefully understated. I have come to view his smoke-screen strategy as part of a more generalized pattern in his writing that takes various verbal, syntactic, and structural forms. The strategy is designed to conceal his meanings in areas touching his deep-seated beliefs, yet permit revealing glimpses. It keeps a little back, leaves some ideas unsaid. But its underlying impulse is not grudging; it rises above the mere inclination to be taciturn. Some years ago I designated this quality in Frost as "reserve"—a term that acknowledges his need for privacy and his desire to keep some meanings in store, reserved. ("Reserve in the Art of Robert Frost," *The Texas Quarterly*, Summer 1963.) These meanings are imbedded in the language, the metaphors, of the poetry—withheld from the casual reader, but at least partly available to the diligent.

"How do we know," I once heard Frost ask rhetorically, "when someone is hinting at something or speaking straight goods?" "Only among the best of friends," he said, "can we speak straight goods." (Even his letters to close friends, though, were not free of those "smoke screens.") He continued to muse about the right to emotional self-protection; then focusing his ramblings into a crescendo, he proclaimed that he wouldn't write his own biography —"I'd lie!" His voice dropped and he added, "Don't trust me. Trust the poems."

This advice is not so easy to follow as Frost was making it seem, for he was a master of verbal acrobatics. He loved the richness of language and had fun playing with words—shifting dramatic tone, dodging, hedging, qualifying, and reversing syntactic direction. In and out of poetry he avoided being pinned down. He didn't like to meet a question head-on. He had often named Emerson as a literary figure he much admired, and I once asked whether he meant *as philosopher* or *as poet*? He rejected my alternatives, yet his answer was right on target: "Emerson is a real poet in prose or verse." Later the same evening he was talking about the importance of seeing *into* something, seeing *through* something. Someone wanted to know, "How do you penetrate a poem you don't understand?" Rabbi-like, answering a question with another question, he rejoined, "How do you penetrate a lunkhead?" Having gained the advantage, he boasted, "I like to think I'm up to most things. If I don't understand a poem, somebody's to blame, and it's *not me!*" Another time he fended off the presumption of a "don't-you" type question, "I think to bear life one has to believe in God, don't you?" by diverting the issue: "There's a lot of pain in the world." He refused to speak to the point, but what he said was not really off the point either.

Such evasive tactics in Frost's repartee were rooted in the same protective impulse that governed his poetic technique. Indeed this impulse had early solidified into an aesthetic principle—as we learn in a 1929 letter to Sidney Cox:

> A little of anything goes a long way in art. Im [*sic*] never so desperate for material that I have to trench on the confidential for one thing, nor on the private for another nor on the personal, nor in general on the sacred.

The letter sets a limit to the *expression* theory of art:

> Poetry is measured in more senses than one: it is measured feet but more important still it is a measured amount of all we could say an [if] we would. We shall be judged finally by the delicacy of our feeling of where to stop short. . . . There is no greater fallacy going than that art is expression—an undertaking to tell all to the last scrapings of the brain pan.

Late in his life, to a Bread Loaf audience, Frost talked again of "delicacy," referring to "the line of delicacy" in poetry, and it was clear he felt he had held close to it in his own work. "I've written a whole book," he observed, "without the word *sex* in it. That doesn't mean I've left anything out." He was aware, no doubt, of sexual undercurrents in the imagery of "Putting in the Seed," "A Hillside Thaw," and less subtly, "The Subverted Flower." Perhaps he played a private joke about birds-and-bees beneath the reverent surface of "A Prayer in Spring." Like passion, tragedy in the poetry is held in check by the discipline of artistic form. Think, for example, of the fragile beauty of "Spring Pools" whose

"flowery waters" are imperiled by the "pent-up" destructive power of innocuous leaf-buds. Or remember the murderous violence in
"The Vanishing Red," shown to the reader only by deduction; and
the sudden, stark but brief picture of physical mutilation in " 'Out,
Out—.' " Many of Frost's poems have a simplicity a child can
grasp; others look into an abyss of terror or deal in complexities
that would confound a sage. While his language is never esoteric,
his meanings often plumb fathomless depths. He had no personal
place for stylistic abstruseness, nor patience with it. At Yale
University in 1961, skirting the question of darkness, of terror, in
"Spring Pools," he added:

> Some people don't know the difference between obscurity and
> what are called in ancient times "dark sayings"—that you go into
> deeper and darker in your life. But obscurity isn't that. Obscurity
> usually is a cover for nothing. You go looking for it and it comes out
> "a stitch in time saves nine," or something like that. But there are
> "dark sayings."

Though stylistically lucid, Frost's poetry is a record of a lifetime
spent digging "deeper and darker" into the mysteries of existence.

Frost himself matched the deceptive simplicity of his poetry. "I
have not known," Sidney Cox wrote of him, "a more complex
person, though I have not known one so nearly simple." The once
popular image of Frost as witty cracker-barrel philosopher has
now been modified, at least among serious students of his poetry.
But the more we come to understand him, the more, paradoxi-
cally, he eludes us. He eludes through contradiction. He exhibits
the banter and acerbity of a Twain; he contains the tragic depths
of a Sophocles. He is the common-sensical realist, and he is—it
may surprise some—part mystic. (His heritage, very likely, from
his Swedenborgian mother.) To watch him say his poems was to
witness this curious mystical quality. Some recordings of his poetry readings capture his quick-witted asides which spark errati-
cally in all directions, as if fed by the very fire that set the poems
aglow. Yet the recordings cannot capture the visionary flame,
clear and steady, burning within his deep blue eyes. Mark Harris,
interviewing him in 1961 for *Life* magazine, explained it this way:
"Somewhere behind his eyes Mr. Frost was hiding."

On rare occasions Robert Frost, like the ground hog looking for its shadow on the second of February, edged warily into the open. "This word *God*," he told Harris in the interview, "is not an often used word with me, but once in a while it arrives there." He never stayed out of cover for long though. In the idiom of the drumlin woodchuck of his poem, he was "so instinctively thorough/About [his] crevice and burrow." Verbal ambiguity was one camouflage; humor, another. He acknowledges the protective value of irony and humor in a 1924 letter to Louis Untermeyer:

> Irony is simply a kind of guardedness. So is a twinkle. It keeps the reader from criticism. . . . Belief is better than anything else, and it is best when rapt, above paying its respects to anybody's doubt whatsoever. At bottom the world isn't a joke. We only joke about it to avoid an issue with someone to let someone know that we know he's there with his questions: to disarm him by seeming to have heard and done justice to his side of the standing argument. Humor is the most engaging cowardice. With it myself I have been able to hold some of my enemy in play far out of gunshot.

These remarks suggest that Frost hid his "belief" to keep it from being challenged by the non-believer. (Lawrance Thompson makes a case for this theory in his biography of the poet.) Sometimes he did let down his guard, as in an earlier letter (1921) to Untermeyer where he confides, "I shouldn't wonder if my last end would be religious." This sentiment was evidently prophetic, for his deathbed letter (12 January 1963) to Roy and Alma Elliott reminisces about old times and returns to an apparently lifelong concern with the question of divine justice, mercy, and salvation:

> Why will the quidnuncs always be hoping for a salvation man will never have from anyone but God? I was just saying today how Christ posed Himself the whole problem and died for it. How can we be just in a world that needs mercy and merciful in a world that needs justice. We study and study the four biographies of Him and are left still somewhat puzzled in our daily lives. Marking students in a kind of mockery and laughing it off. It seems as if I never wrote these plunges into the depths to anyone but you. I remember our first walk to Harpswell together. . . . If only I get well . . . I'll go deeper into my life with you than I ever have before.

The spiritual probing in this letter is, not too surprisingly, altogether absent in Frost's reply a month earlier to an interviewer's
query about his vigorous good health. (As it happened, the interview took place just two weeks before he underwent minor
surgery. Soon after, in a weakened condition, he contracted
pneumonia and died.) What he said was terse and stoic:

> I guess I don't take life very seriously. It's hard to get into this world
> and hard to get out of it. And what's in between doesn't make much
> sense. If that sounds pessimistic, let it stand. There's been too much
> vaporous optimism voiced about life and age. Maybe this will pro-
> vide a little balance.[2]

The distinct contrast between religious preoccupation in the
deathbed letter and bald unsentimentality in the interview response should not affect our assessment of the poet's belief.
Rather, the contrast is indicative of stylistic adjustments he chose
to make, depending upon his audience. The letter is full of spiritual pondering; the interview avoids any speculation about the
consolations of religion. To his friends he is confidential; to the
reporter he is nonchalant, impersonal. With cool mental agility he
refuses to be swept away on a tide of rhetoric.

The kind of audience he confronted, it seems, was only one
factor determining the degree of reticence he exercised. Shifting
moods also governed his behavior. Theodore Morrison tells how
the poet's temperamental pendulum swung:

> When the mood was on him, he could spill out confidences with a
> recklessness the very opposite of the man who made himself a
> place apart and hid his tracks by teasing and flouting.[3]

Morrison's language ("teasing," "flouting") echoes the early poem
"Revelation" with its hide-and-seek metaphor, an image which
becomes a key to interpreting all of Robert Frost. The incongruities in the personality are matched by tensions and ambiguities in
the poetry. Critics looking for some coherent philosophical
framework, some intellectual scaffold for religious belief, are
often baffled by both poetry and person. Some, dismayed, judge
him an agnostic. A particularly knotty problem arises from the

fact that he is noncommittal on the subject of religion. Yet he is not spiritually *un*committed. Belief is a central concern in his work and the driving force behind it.

One more point about *afterimagery*. Frost may have borrowed the term from the technical discipline of psychology, but he extended its meaning beyond. He plays with its religious connotations, if not with the word itself, in "After Apple-Picking." In the field of aesthetics, J. McBride Dabbs gives us Frost's observation as to the limits of poetic thinking: "Imagery and after-imagery are about all there is to poetry. Synecdoche and synecdoche." A parallel idea is found in his maxim (quoted by Dabbs): "Sight and insight are the whole business of the poet." (*"Ex*cite, too," he once added.) To him, poetry consisted primarily of *seeing*—perceiving the physical image, and *seeing into*—conceiving the mental afterimage. There the poetic process stops, for "something must be left to God."

The process might be thought of as a balancing of pairs: sight and insight; perception and conception; image and afterimage. Or, more accurately, as transformational—a dynamic interaction between the sensory faculties and the intellectual-emotional-psychic. Put simply, it is the way man comes to know the world. This idea is made explicit in a talk Frost delivered at Amherst College titled "Education by Poetry"—published in the *Amherst Graduates' Quarterly* of February 1931. "Education by poetry," he said, "is education by metaphor."

> I have wanted in late years to go further and further in making metaphor the whole of thinking. I find some one now and then to agree with me that all thinking, except mathematical thinking, is metaphorical, or all thinking except scientific thinking. The mathematical might be difficult for me to bring in, but the scientific is easy enough.

He went on to explain that scientific theory has always been metaphoric. "Once on a time all the Greeks were busy telling each other what the All was—or was like unto. All was three elements, air, earth, and water . . . . All was substance, said another. All was change, said a third. But best and most fruitful was Pythago-

ras' comparison of the universe with number." Modern science
has hit upon a new metaphor to describe the universe:

> "In the neighborhood of matter space is something like curved."
> Isn't that a good one! It seems to me that that is simply and utterly
> charming—to say that space is something like curved in the neigh-
> borhood of matter. "Something like."

Frost's point was that modern scientists, like their predecessors
(more often called philosophers), "busy" themselves getting up
cosmic metaphors, and he extolled their efforts. "Greatest of all
attempts to say one thing in terms of another is the philosophical
attempt to say matter in terms of spirit, or spirit in terms of matter,
to make the final unity." The peak performance of metaphor is in
the reaching of the mind for ultimate knowledge, when metaphor
aspires to link physical existence to spiritual essence. He conceded, however, "That is the greatest attempt that ever failed. We
stop just short there."

The thoughts he offered in the thirties at Amherst resonate in an
offhand comment he made three decades later, in his last summer
at Bread Loaf: "All metaphor breaks down somewhere. The trick
is to know how far you can carry it before it breaks." Listening, I
wondered if the limitation recognized in this casual remark might
be one more way of leaving "something . . . to God"—an acknowledgment of the deity's claim to secrecy beyond the scope of
human images and afterimages. I was beginning to see that, for
Frost, *reserve* was a universal phenomenon. Or, metaphorically
speaking, "the All . . . was like unto" a Secret ("The Secret
Sits"):

> We dance round in a ring and suppose,
> But the Secret sits in the middle and knows.

II

Trusting in Contraries

*It must be the brook
Can trust itself to go by contraries
The way I can with you—and you with me—*

—"WEST-RUNNING BROOK"

"ONE MORE BREVITY"

The term *reserve*, we have seen, is comprehensive. It defines Frost's life-style and his artistic style. It bears upon his religious belief; it has cosmic implications. Not surprisingly, variations on the theme of reserve recur throughout his poetry. The variants may involve reserving certain prerogatives to the deity. They may suggest reserving judgment for a period of time—or altogether upon this earth, until, as Frost put it, "the final returns are in." They may focus on reticence in communication, or on concealment in the process of revelation—both human and divine. "A Prayer in Spring," which stylistically demonstrates *reserve as tact*, thematically treats *reserve as cosmic scheme*. The poem views human love *sub specie aeternitatis*. The passion of sexual intercourse— delicately implied in the images of dilating bee swarm and hummingbird's thrust—is a partial fulfillment of divine love:

> And make us happy in the happy bees,
> The swarm dilating round the perfect trees.
>
> And make us happy in the darting bird
> That suddenly above the bees is heard,
> The meteor that thrusts in with needle bill,
> And off a blossom in mid air stands still.
>
> For this is love and nothing else is love,
> The which it is reserved for God above
> To sanctify to what far ends He will,
> But which it only needs that we fulfill.

Most surely a "love poem" (recall that Frost said, "All my poems are love poems"), "A Prayer in Spring" places human love in a metaphysical context. The natural rhythms of bird and bees affirm the essential innocence of physical passion. The poem avoids prudery by recognizing sex as part of the order of things. But human love, while good, is incomplete; its sanctification is "reserved for God."

This early poem from *A Boy's Will* introduces motifs that turn up repeatedly in Frost's later work. One is the idea that in some mysterious way mankind collaborates in a universal design. Another is the notion—it gains the status of conviction—that man must act from only partial knowledge, but always out of faith in a larger meaning. Frost's stress is upon action, not upon theorizing. Another motif is that of love as a counterforce to the passage of time. The "darting bird" that "in mid air stands still" suggests capturing *in time* an instant of eternity, by a surge of feeling—not by intellect. At the moment of sexual consummation there is a fleeting sense of the timeless. The image anticipates a later poem, "The Master Speed" (an epithalamion for Frost's daughter Marjorie), where love thwarts time; here, through their love, the bridal pair may " . . . in the rush of everything to waste,/ . . . have the power of standing still." Similarly, in "West-Running Brook" human love is a "strange resistance" to "The universal cataract of death"—a resistance that is hinted to be "sacred." Finally, "A Prayer in Spring," despite its clear joyousness, reflects Frost's early awareness of the darker side of existence. The poem celebrates springtime; it petitions for youthful bliss: "keep us here/All simply in the springing of the year." Yet innocence must yield at last to wisdom. A time "far away" may disclose "the uncertain harvest" that lies ahead.[1]

The idea of man's reserving certain prerogatives for God is found also in "Good-by and Keep Cold." Here the fate of an apple orchard which must be abandoned to the winter snows is entrusted to "God." The end of the poem returns the contracted "Good-by" in the title to its etymological root—"God be with ye":

> I wish I could promise to lie in the night
> And think of an orchard's arboreal plight
> When slowly (and nobody comes with a light)
> Its heart sinks lower under the sod.
> But something has to be left to God.

Other Frost poems treat *reserve as concealment*, reserve as counterbalance to the urge for communication. Frost's personality was anomalous and his poetry abounds in paradox. Characteristically reticent, he could occasionally, as noted, broadcast confidences wholesale. Like the stream in "West-Running Brook," he could "trust [himself] to go by contraries"; one might even assert that he went *only* by contraries—and to heap an apparent contradiction upon all the rest, he was nevertheless extremely consistent.

Frost's personal impulses toward confidentiality, on the one hand, and divulging secrets, on the other, find near-parallels at a philosophical level. Just as he invested the right of reserve with moral implications, so also was he aware, especially as artist, of a moral obligation to communicate. Speaking of "the fear of Man" (in his 1935 Introduction to Edwin Arlington Robinson's *King Jasper*), he explains that there is "the fear that men won't understand us and we shall be cut off from them." (In the essay he juxtaposes this fear with "the fear of God.") Likewise, his poem "The Fear of Man" ends:

> May I in my brief bolt across the scene
> Not be misunderstood in what I mean.

The metaphoric vehicle here is the homeward journey of a young girl "at midnight from a friend's." Just preceding the lines quoted above, the poem reads:

> Her fear is being spoken by the rude
> And having her exposure misconstrued.

The girl is, figuratively, virginal poetry—not to be defiled by insensitive readers. These final couplets embody the essence of Frost's dilemma as artist: how to reconcile communication and reserve, how to reach the sensitized reader and eschew the shallow-minded, the reader who would reduce a valid ambiguity to a false simplicity. Like the girl's virginity, the integrity of a poem must be preserved—in reality, and for the sake of reputation.

Frost's solution to the artistic dilemma lay in a recognition that communication of metaphoric meaning must risk being reserved from some so that it can more faithfully be transmitted to others. Thus the impulses of communication and of reserve ultimately function as interdependent tensions. The integrity of a poem lies in keeping intact its multiple meanings. To preserve this integrity— to let nothing escape—a poet is often complex, oblique, ambiguous. As Frost saw the dilemma, a poet must run the risk of cutting off communication altogether, since it is better to be *un-*

understood (by some) than—through a deceptive simplification of meaning—*mis*understood (by all).

For Frost successful communication between poet and reader was a matter of emotional and intellectual interaction. A "correspondence," he felt, exists at both verbal and non-verbal levels; his *King Jasper* Introduction explains:

> We began in infancy by establishing correspondence of eyes with eyes. We recognized that they were the same feature and we could do the same things with them. We went on to the visible motion of the lips—smile answered smile; then cautiously, by trial and error, to compare the invisible muscles of the mouth and throat. They were the same and could make the same sounds. . . . From here on the wonder grows. It has been said that recognition in art is all. Better say correspondence is all. Mind must convince mind that it can uncurl and wave the same filaments of subtlety, soul convince soul that it can give off the same shimmers of eternity.

An "infant," from the Latin derivation, is one who does not yet speak. So the infant begins with other means of communication. Readers familiar with Frost's "All Revelation" may seize upon a connection between our first mode of correspondence, "in infancy," and the image, "Eyes seeking the response of eyes." More about this point later on. A much earlier poem, a companion piece, "Revelation," is pertinent to the present discussion.

Frost extended his concept of the interdependence of communication and reserve to the entire realm of nature, and (figuratively, at least) to the supernatural, for God and poet are both "makers" —players with metaphor. "Revelation" toys with the idea of a divine hide-and-seek game:

> We make ourselves a place apart
>   Behind light words that tease and flout,
> But oh, the agitated heart
>   Till someone really find us out.
>
> 'Tis pity if the case require
>   (Or so we say) that in the end

> We speak the literal to inspire
>   The understanding of a friend.
>
> But so with all, from babes that play
>   At hide-and-seek to God afar,
> So all who hide too well away
>   Must speak and tell us where they are.

The final stanza enlarges the human problem (particularly, one guesses, the artist's) of concealing and revealing, by projecting it upon the deity. Admittedly, playfulness here precludes our putting much stock in any theological implications. Look, though, at the later "All Revelation" which treats a parallel theme with considerable seriousness and complexity. The underlying argument there is essentially compatible with that in this early *jeu d'esprit*.

"Choose Something Like a Star" also flirts with the notion of communication between man and whatever there may be supernatural in the universe. Here the dog-star, Sirius,[2] displays petulant ambivalence toward mankind. The man in the poem grants the star a modicum of "reserve," but gently chides nonetheless:

> O Star (the fairest one in sight),
> We grant your loftiness the right
> To some obscurity of cloud—
> It will not do to say of night,
> Since dark is what brings out your light.
> Some mystery becomes the proud.
> But to be wholly taciturn
> In your reserve is not allowed.

The star, proving "taciturn," says merely " 'I burn' "; "But does tell something in the end":

> And steadfast as Keats' Eremite,
> Not even stooping from its sphere,
> It asks a little of us here.
> It asks of us a certain height,
> So when at times the mob is swayed
> To carry praise or blame too far,
> We may choose something like a star
> To stay our minds on and be staid.

Concealment and revelation are presented as inherent universal principles. Without darkness there is no starlight; metaphorically, without mystery, no vision. The poem is aspiratory: upward gazing eyes seek correspondence with a star; the reaching mind yearns for "shimmers of eternity."[3]

In "Revelation" God is in hiding; in "Choose Something Like a Star" nature keeps its own counsel. Turning the tables, Frost once asked, "If God and nature can have secrets, why can't a poet?" "One More Brevity," a not-so-brief poem in his final volume, is probably Frost's most extensive treatment of the right of reserve at various levels of creation, all but one of them—man—nonverbal. The narrative involves a nocturnal visit of an ordinary canine "Gus," who undergoes a fancied metamorphosis in the course of the plot, into some sort of heavenly messenger— possibly Sirius. Strategic shifts of tone throughout hint at meanings, but stop short of disclosure.

The opening lines suggest man's preoccupation with pursuing meanings and the limitations the universe sets to man's quest:

> I opened the door so my last look
> Should be taken outside a house and book.
> Before I gave up seeing and slept
> I said I would see how Sirius kept
> His watch-dog eye on what remained
> To be gone into if not explained.

The phrases "my last look" and "gave up seeing and slept" point toward the idea of man's mortality and begin the poem in a serious key. Man would seem obliged to probe the mystery of existence, but he must not expect total enlightenment; his *seeing* is only partial.

The abrupt intrusion in the next lines of "an earthly dog of the carriage breed" shifts our attention from the cosmic to the domestic, from the serious to the comic:

> He dumped himself like a bag of bones,
> He sighed himself a couple of groans,
> And head to tail then firmly curled
> Like swearing off on the traffic world.

This "problem guest," the poem insists, is "Not a heavenly dog made manifest"—an assumption it would not have occurred to the reader to make had it not been denied. The denial is further reinforced with the resonance of concrete reality:

> His hard tail loudly smacked the floor

The hint at the dog's mysterious origin is followed up with homely sentiment:

> As if beseeching me, "Please, no more,
> I can't explain—tonight at least."
> His brow was perceptibly trouble-creased.

The host responds with assurance of his guest's prerogative of privacy:

> "Gustie, old boy, Dalmatian Gus,
> You're right, there's nothing to discuss.
> Don't try to tell me what's on your mind,
> The sorrow of having been left behind,
> Or the sorrow of having run away.
> All that can wait for the light of day."

The phrase "light of day" provides a momentary link with the philosophical implications of the opening lines—suggesting the end of mortal vision and ultimate clarification hereafter. The poem continues with further confirmation to the canine visitor of the right of reserve:

> "Meanwhile feel obligation-free.
> Nobody has to confide in me."

The tone of moral earnestness is interrupted then with a wry acknowledgment of the comic limitations of the situation:

> 'Twas too one-sided a dialogue,
> And I wasn't sure I was talking dog.

The first long stanza then ends on a domestic note which opens into larger meaning:

> I broke off baffled. But all the same,
> In fancy, I ratified his name,
> Gustie, Dalmatian Gus, that is,
> And started shaping my life to his,
> Finding him in his right supplies
> And sharing his miles of exercise.

The question of tone in these lines is evocative. In general, we might call them gentle and mildly amused at a recognition of changes the dog's presence would make in his host's routine. But there is a faint suggestion of something more cogent in the phrase "started shaping my life to his"—the sense perhaps of a claim upon the host's life, not from a lowlier, but from a higher order of being.

The second stanza builds slowly from a mundane beginning to an enigmatic climax which effectually reverses the earlier disclaimer of Gus's super-canine character. Morning has come and the dog leaves as unexpectedly as he had arrived:

> Next morning the minute I was about
> He was at the door to be let out
> With an air that said, "I have paid my call.
> You mustn't feel hurt if now I'm all
> For getting back somewhere or further on."
> I opened the door and he was gone.

Both stanzas start with an opening of the door. What can we say of the ordinary-extraordinary night that intervenes? Gus's destination, like his origin, is unexplained and unexplored, yet he responds in a purposeful ("I have paid my call"), if vague ("back somewhere or further on"), manner. In the first stanza he is greeted as truant "Who, having failed of the modern speed,/Now asked asylum." Traditionally a carriage dog for horse-drawn fire engines, he has not adjusted to the mechanized world. He suffers, perhaps, "The sorrow of having been left behind"—like God in *A Masque of Reason* whose "forte is truth,/ . . . /While science goes self-superseding on." In the second stanza he seems more pursuitist than escapist, remembering "the sorrow of having run away." Might "Dalmatian Gus" be a milder mannered relative of the divine "Hound of Heaven" who dogs Jonah's flight in *A*

Masque of Mercy?[4] To press the dog-God metaphor, is Gus bound backward to beginnings or impelled forward to some end? His in-difference suggests the interchangeability of directions—like alpha and omega coming full-circle.

As in the earlier stanza, the theme of mortality is again introduced—appropriately, since "One More Brevity" is a dis-guised elegy for Gillie, Frost's Border collie.[5] Gus's departure triggers melancholy speculation in the forsaken host:

> I was to taste in little the grief
> That comes of dogs' lives being so brief,
> Only a fraction of ours at most.

Suddenly sorrow gives way to eeriness:

> He might have been the dream of a ghost
> In spite of the way his tail had smacked
> My floor so hard and matter-of-fact.

Juxtaposing "dream" and "fact," Frost—with deft sleight-of-mind—dissipates into fancy what had seemed "hard" reality. The poem then escalates to the miraculous:

> And things have been going so strangely since
> I wouldn't be too hard to convince,
> I might even claim, he was Sirius
> (Think of presuming to call him Gus)
> The star itself, Heaven's greatest star,
> Not a meteorite, but an avatar,
> Who had made an overnight descent
> To show by deeds he didn't resent
> My having depended on him so long,
> And yet done nothing about it in song.

The "claim" is cast, guardedly, in the conditional mode, but sweeping rhetoric, as the passage mounts to a climax, far over-powers any grammatical modesty.

After this extravagance the poem retreats once more to under-statement and closes by reiterating the principle of reserve. The right to withhold meanings which had been accorded his visitor, the host concludes by taking for himself:

A symbol was all he could hope to convey,
A intimation, a shot of ray,
A meaning I was supposed to seek,
And finding, wasn't disposed to speak.

"One More Brevity" opens with a man's taking a "last look" at the night sky—at things to be gazed at, but not "explained"—and closes with a hint of some tiny ray-like enlightenment. (We can picture the cathode ray in "All Revelation" which activates the inner crystals of the geode to luminescence.) Yet the man, finally, reverts to the non-verbal, not "disposed to speak." Language, we must guess, is inadequate for embodying mystery. In Frost's poetry, subtly but pervasively, there is a dichotomy between speech and vision, between saying and seeing. As he remarked in 1961 at Bread Loaf, "Poets aren't supposed to tell what it is they see." But even poets (in Saint Paul's phrase) "see through a glass, darkly." Thinking of a more nearly perfect vision hereafter, Frost ended the last line of his poem "The Strong Are Saying Nothing" with a confident "until they see." No doubt he expected the gap to close "beyond the grave."

For all its whimsicality "One More Brevity" underscores a conviction that recurs in Robert Frost's thinking: that the more concrete the reality, the more mysterious it is. He once observed that "a romanticist and a realist both fall in love for what they *don't* know." "But," he continued, "the realist falls in love with the *less obvious* mystery, the *more mysterious* mystery." That Gus is an ordinary carriage dog whose "hard tail loudly smacked the floor" makes him all the more, not less, mysterious. Frost's vision is that of a realist who includes a dimension of mystery in his definition of reality—a realist who searches stone walls for fallen meteorites, as in "A Star in a Stone-Boat," and rock geodes for their inner crystals, as in "All Revelation."

In "One More Brevity"—and elsewhere—Frost plays with the *idea* of God. The reader would be misguided to identify such play-with-an-idea with a *belief* in God. The act of play, though, had for Frost distinct religious significance and it would be equally erroneous to suppose that playfulness precludes belief. "One More Brevity" draws upon Hindu thought, presumably to avoid the more familiar (to the Western world) Judeo-Christian concept of divinity. The poem introduces the idea of God in Eastern terminology; *avatar* is a divine incarnation associated chiefly with Vishnu. Its approximate equivalent in Western theology is *saviour*. Even if Frost's language urges us toward the Veda, it is Gus's ambivalent personality—pursuitist/escapist, revealer/concealer—that returns us to the God of Isaiah (45:15): "Verily thou art a God that hidest thyself, O God of Israel, the Saviour." We are brought back in Frost's poetry to the God of Job and of Moses, to the mysterious Jehovah of whirlwind and burning bush—a God of conundrums.

Throughout, He is a God who is for the most part hidden. In "Sitting by a Bush in Broad Sunlight" He is presented figuratively as having assumed the veil and vowed silence, like a nun:

> God once declared he was true
> And then took the veil and withdrew,
> And remember how final a hush
> Then descended of old on the bush.

The poem refers, of course, to Yahweh's appearance to Moses in the burning bush on Mount Horeb (Exodus, 3:4 ff.). (Another reference to the burning bush occurs in *A Masque of Reason*.) In the Biblical story, Yahweh shows—even when confronting Moses—a furtive tendency. Moses' question as to His name receives a cryptic reply: "I AM THAT I AM: . . . Thus shalt thou say unto the children of Israel, I AM hath sent me unto you."

The Old Testament taboo about naming the deity seems to lurk behind Frost's reticence to speak of God. "Truth," too, in his poems is treated cautiously. It is elusive, or at times illusory, lying, as Democritus felt, at the bottom of a deep well ("For Once, Then, Something"). The veiling of "Truth" yields a variety of images, often involving barriers between man and nature: "a tumbled wall" ("Two Look at Two"), "window glass" ("Questioning Faces"). Moments of communion nevertheless do exist in Frost—between man and the natural, perhaps the supernatural, realm. The wall, after all, is "tumbled"; glass is transparent. As from a speeding train window, we catch, at times, "A Passing Glimpse":

> Heaven gives its glimpses only to those
> Not in position to look too close.

These rare moments are characteristically non-rational, non-verbal. They cut beneath intellectual understanding to a more primitive level of awareness. They are *gifts* (instants of grace?)—either to children or to man when he becomes as a child or to man when he journeys backward—symbolically and psychologically—to his human origins, or to the beginnings of creation.

III

Grace Notes

And then we were vouchsafed the miracle
That never yet to other two befell
And I alone of us have lived to tell.

—"IRIS BY NIGHT"

"LOOKING FOR A SUNSET BIRD IN WINTER"

An insistent strain of skepticism, to be sure, is heard throughout Frost's poetry. But a tone of reverence, low-keyed and pervasive, is audible, too. Theodore Morrison has said of the spiritual quality in the poetry:

> Everyone who reads Frost feels, I suppose, that in some sense he was a deeply religious man, if only in the sense that his poems are emotionally charged with an ultimate piety.[1]

What gives the poems this sustained measure of piety? I think it comes partly from a quality of heart and mind uniquely attuned to what Frost himself called "nature's favors"—fleeting moments of particular magic and wonder that man encounters in nature. Frost's poetry captures many such moments, where "inner" and "outer . . . weather" converge with a sense of immediacy, causing psychological or spiritual modulation. It is of their essence that they are, on nature's side, unheralded, and, on man's side, unexpected and unearned. In the language of "The Death of the Hired Man," they are "Something you somehow haven't to deserve." Some such moments are decidedly naturalistic, involving a change in the landscape—either fancied or real—that brings a transitory lift of spirits. In "A Boundless Moment" an optical trick turns windy March into flowering May; a deceptive glimpse of "the Paradise-in-Bloom" out of season is soon recognized as "A young beech clinging to its last year's leaves." The psychological uplift, while rooted in illusion, is nevertheless valid. Other moments of "favor," however, produce a change more subtle, more intense, more mysterious. At its extreme ("Iris by Night") this kind of transformation seems to carry the viewer to a mystical plane where he is absorbed into the landscape. Less extreme instances ("Two Look at Two"; "Stopping by Woods") convey a spiritual rapport with nature that stops short of identification. Sometimes mere fancy is a touchstone to mystery: a cold stone may once have been a shooting star ("A Star in a Stone-Boat").

A number of natural favors occur in *New Hampshire* (1923), in the third section of that volume, titled "Grace Notes." Frost's name for the section suggests that he wanted the poems in it to serve as a graceful counterpoint to the *tour-de-force* title narrative of the first section and the mock-scholarly "Notes" of the second. (He playfully devised cross-references from the title poem to poems of the "Notes" section, presumably as a parody of T. S. Eliot's elaborate annotation of *The Waste Land*, published the previous year.) Like musical grace notes, the poems furnish ornamental embellishment. In music, grace notes do not keep the regular beat of the score; the moments recorded in these poems are inserted into time, but their essence is apart from it. And to the extent that they carry the notion of unmerited gift, they are in yet another way "graced." One, "Stopping by Woods on a Snowy Evening"—we know from Frost's account of its composition—is a "grace note" in a further sense. He relates having stayed up all night working on the lengthy "New Hampshire"; when the sun rose, the short graceful lyric about "The darkest evening of the year" came to him virtually intact. Its technically demanding rhyme pattern (linking each stanza to the preceding) is emblematic of a night of arduous dedication to the longer poem. Yet the lyric itself *seems* effortless.

In and out of *New Hampshire* there are poems embodying moments of natural favor, or grace. "Questioning Faces," in the final volume, captures an instant of unexpected felicity:

> The winter owl banked just in time to pass
> And save herself from breaking window glass.
> And her wings straining suddenly aspread
> Caught color from the last of evening red
> In a display of underdown and quill
> To glassed-in children at the window sill.

Though first published in 1958 in *The Saturday Review*, the poem is almost certainly based on a favor Frost remembered from his Franconia years (1915-1920) when, as Reginald Cook paraphrases the poet's recollection:

> as he sat by a farmhouse window looking at a brilliant sunset, suddenly an owl appeared, banked against the window and dropped away. Briefly he glimpsed the owl's wing-quills and the downy breast feathers.[2]

Cook recalls that Frost said he felt as if he had been "spoken to—favored."

"Questioning Faces" preserves a memory so vivid that it survived several decades, yet in the poem the impact of the event is left to inference. Brilliant color and vibrant energy dramatize the inherent wonder of a split second in time; the owl banks in flight at just the right angle to the setting sun, and at the exact instant when the children happen to be watching. Propitious timing, which must seem coincidental, and a motiveless simplicity lie at the heart of moments of grace.

The adoption of the children's point of view, rather than the more customary adult first person, is curious (especially since the genesis of the poem is probably autobiographical) and worth exploring. Their perspective of innocence, perhaps, permits an unintellectualized immediacy of vision. We recall Christ's admonition to his disciples that they become as "little children" to "receive the kingdom of God." The children's "questioning" is non-verbal, non-rational. Such a concept of truth, not as too complex for man's intellect, but as too incomprehensibly simple occurs elsewhere in Frost's poetry. When Job, in *A Masque of Reason*, learns in the afterworld that his earthly ordeal was a matter of God's "just showing off to the Devil," he feels let down. "I expected," Job reflects, "more/Than I could understand and what I get/Is almost less than I can understand." Similarly, in "Directive," the Grail-like "drinking goblet" has been stolen "from the *children's* playhouse" and "kept hidden . . . so the wrong ones can't find it,/So can't get saved, as Saint Mark says they mustn't." And the metaphoric "road" to salvation in "Directive" is through a landscape "made *simple* by the loss/Of detail." (Italics mine.)

For motiveless simplicity "Dust of Snow" is virtually unmatched among Frost's poems. Surely a "brevity"—two dimeter quatrains a single sentence in length—it captures a moment of psychic renewal:

> The way a crow
> Shook down on me
> The dust of snow
> From a hemlock tree

Has given my heart
A change of mood
And saved some part
Of a day I had rued.

The unexpectedly beneficent snow-dusting is a kind of naturalistic baptismal rite in which emotional rebirth is freely "given." But the favor is accidental. As in "Questioning Faces," the instant of grace depends on propinquity. The feeling of correspondence with nature exists at a non-rational, psychic level. Not the dusting itself, but "The way" it happens, works the inner "change." "The way" is not specified; it is not a matter for inquiry.

The genealogy of title for "Dust of Snow" reveals some verbal connections in Frost's thinking and indicates an initial pressure of the religious upon the secular. Its earliest known title in a 1920 typescript is "A Mercy." In its first printing, in England, later the same year it appeared as "A Favour," and immediately thereafter, in the United States, as "Snow Dust." By the time of its publication in *New Hampshire* the title had come to rest as "Dust of Snow."[3]

The transition from "A Mercy" to "A Favour" implies a disinclination for the religious stamp. While the direction in the variant titles is toward the secular, and ultimately to the neutral ground of the purely descriptive, we can infer—since "Dust of Snow" is one of the *New Hampshire* "Grace Notes"—a verbal matrix in Frost's thought involving *mercy, grace,* and *favor.* To this grouping we may add *gift*; the snow-dusting is coincidental, but it is received as a gift. Likewise, Silas' refuge ("The Death of the Hired Man") did not have to be deserved. Jonah—in the masque dealing with "mercy"—seeks asylum in "a gift shop." And, in "Looking for a Sunset Bird in Winter," the bird's song is "an angelic gift," a freely given talent.

The "Sunset Bird" poem uses both illusory and real natural effects to produce a heightened state of awareness. The initial premise is fairly ordinary: a man treks homeward in a winter twilight across a silent white terrain. But an apparition—something he "thought" he saw—brings back, in stanza two, evensong from summer landscapes. A dramatic tension is established between delightful fantasy and cold reality:

The west was getting out of gold,
The breath of air had died of cold,
When shoeing home across the white,
I thought I saw a bird alight.

In summer when I passed the place
I had to stop and lift my face;
A bird with an angelic gift
Was singing in it sweet and swift.

Here, as in "A Boundless Moment," an optical trick leads to an imagined seasonal change, a brief psychological lift. The recaptured birdsong is evanescent, but its memory gives joy. *Angelic* may be merely a superlative, indicating exquisite melody. The scene tempts us, however, to hear, in the musical grace note, religious overtones; the man's uplifted gaze suggests the conventional posture in annunciation portraits, and the bird itself calls to mind the traditional celestial messenger—the Holy Ghost disguised as a dove.

By stanza three the magic moment has passed and the cause of the visual deception, a recalcitrant leaf, is disclosed:

No bird was singing in it now.
A single leaf was on a bough,
And that was all there was to see
In going twice around the tree.

The logic of the situation would now seem complete: an illusion, a triggered memory, the illusion dispelled—from reality to fantasy and back to reality. Some readers may feel that the poem could end here—as "A Boundless Moment," immediately following in *New Hampshire*, ends when the illusion dissolves: "And then I said the truth (and we moved on)." What have the final two stanzas to do with the foregoing three, not just narratively, but thematically?

From my advantage on a hill
I judged that such a crystal chill
Was only adding frost to snow
As gilt to gold that wouldn't show.

A brush had left a crooked stroke
Of what was either cloud or smoke
From north to south across the blue;
A piercing little star was through.

For Frost, thematic integrity within a work was imperative. "Poetic logic," he wrote Louis Untermeyer, " . . . is the thing I set above all things in poetry." To sense the unity of "Sunset Bird" I think we must view it as a sequence of natural favors.

The illusory bird of the first stanza is not, after all, a worthless deception. In this barren winter world it reminds us of the perennial fertility of the earth. The listener, after a flight of fancy, returns to the numbing cold and solitude. He is perhaps more intensely lonely than before, having lost even a *non-existent* bird. But the summer memory has transformed him, sensitized him to the inherent wonder of the slight and transient. His visual acuity now alerts him to the barely perceptible—to ice crystals of frost added to snow (white on white). He is ready for an *actual* moment of grace.

The gold hue of the sky has faded, leaving an indistinct brush stroke across the horizon. The landscape seems (in the metaphor of Emily Dickinson) to hold its breath. Metrically, too, the poem awaits its final line; syntactically the last stanza comes (almost) to rest at the end of its third line, but rhyme and rhythm demand a conclusion. The evening star is climactic, the image gracing the poem as well as the visual scene. It is an appearance, not an apparition. The bird has disappeared around the corner of the seasons. The star appears across light-years of space.

The quality of spiritual elevation in "Looking for a Sunset Bird in Winter" is intense, but subdued. In contrast, "Iris by Night" is suffused with nearly mystical rapture. Like "Two Look at Two," it commemorates a natural favor as well as an intimate human relationship—here Frost's friendship with the British poet Edward Thomas. The two met during Frost's sojourn in England in the teens of the century, and Frost encouraged Thomas as a poet. "Not to Keep" and "A Soldier" are, obliquely, about Thomas. Their friendship is memorialized also in the elegy "To E.T.," written after Thomas had been killed in 1917 at Vimy Ridge in the

British spring offensive. Speaking of this sonnet, Frost wrote to his
Amherst colleague George Whicher in 1919:

> Edward Thomas was the closest friend I ever had and I was the
> closest friend he ever had; and this was something I didn't wait to
> realize after he had died.

To Thomas' widow, Helen, Frost called him "the bravest and best
and dearest man you and I have ever known. . . . you must let
me cry my cry for him as if he were *almost* all mine too."
  For his part, Thomas celebrated the friendship in "The Sun
Used to Shine"; it begins:

> The sun used to shine while we two walked
> Slowly together, paused and started
> Again, and sometimes mused, sometimes talked
> As either pleased, and cheerfully parted . . .

And the rainbow that was to inspire "Iris by Night" is described
by Thomas in a letter to Eleanor Farjeon:

> I like your rainbow, but . . . mine that I saw with Frost seems like
> the first that ever was except that I knew it was a rainbow. I can't
> imagine a painter interfering with either. Mine was too much of a
> pure rainbow, a new toy discovered by Apollo, for anyone to
> paint. It was more for a mythologist clad in skins.[4]

Years later, in 1936, Frost rendered the experience in poetry:

> One misty evening, one another's guide,
> We two were groping down a Malvern side
> The last wet fields and dripping hedges home.
> There came a moment of confusing lights,
> Such as according to belief in Rome
> Were seen of old at Memphis on the heights
> Before the fragments of a former sun
> Could concentrate anew and rise as one.
> Light was a paste of pigment in our eyes.
> And then there was a moon and then a scene
> So watery as to seem submarine;

In which we two stood saturated, drowned.
The clover-mingled rowan on the ground
Had taken all the water it could as dew,
And still the air was saturated too,
Its airy pressure turned to water weight.
Then a small rainbow like a trellis gate,
A very small moon-made prismatic bow,
Stood closely over us through which to go.
And then we were vouchsafed the miracle
That never yet to other two befell
And I alone of us have lived to tell.
A wonder! Bow and rainbow as it bent,
Instead of moving with us as we went,
(To keep the pots of gold from being found)
It lifted from its dewy pediment
Its two mote-swimming many-colored ends,
And gathered them together in a ring.
And we stood in it softly circled round
From all division time or foe can bring
In a relation of elected friends.

Like Thomas' letter, the poem captures the mythic quality of the rainbow, not merely in the title (Iris is the Greek goddess of the rainbow), but in the unearthliness of "the miracle" itself (note the scriptural tone of "vouchsafed"). The scene opens on a still "misty evening" of "wet fields and dripping hedges." There comes a sudden blinding flash of colors, "confusing lights," and then a sense of drowning in a "submarine" atmosphere. Next there appears overhead a "small moon-made prismatic bow"—no ordinary sun-shower rainbow, but a mysterious figment of the night. Presently, an ecstatic transport into the "ring" of the rainbow.

The culminating image—the pair "softly circled round/From all division time or foe can bring"—suggests absolute, eternal unity. We may relate such imagined wholeness of being to the Jungian mandala pattern, one of circular rotation (frequently of rotating light) around a central figure. Traditional religious art forms, of course, place Christ or Buddha within a design of rose or lotus. But Jung recognized the pattern as a manifestation of an archetypally religious attitude, even when it is a projection of what he called "the secular unconscious."[5] Frost's rainbow with "Its two mote-swimming many-colored ends" gathered together symbolizes a mystical oneness into which the "elected friends" are drawn; they are "elected," in the Calvinist meaning, by grace.[6]

The pervasive mystical landscape of "Iris by Night" sets it apart from all Frost's works as a kind of quintessential grace note. The experience that evening on the Malvern hillside should not altogether astonish readers familiar with Frost's latent mysticism and the early Swedenborgian influence from his mother. Thompson's biography records her encouraging her son's gifts of second sight and second hearing, occurrences that terrified him as a boy in San Francisco. And in a 1912 letter quoted by Elizabeth Shepley Sergeant, Frost writes of a Doppelgänger figure in the woods around Plymouth, New Hampshire: "I felt as if I was going to meet my own image in a slanting mirror. Or . . . as if we were two images about to float together with the uncrossing of someone's eyes." "I like a coincidence," he continues, "almost as well as an incongruity." Of all the incongruities in Frost's personality, perhaps the most curious is this mystic current, flowing beneath a solid foundation of Yankee common sense.

IV

A Mercy-Justice Cross

Just an oubliette,
Where you must lie in self-forgetfulness
On the wet flags before a crucifix
I have had painted on the cellar wall
By a religious Aztec Indian.

—A MASQUE OF MERCY

"A MASQUE OF MERCY"

Robert Frost's increasing preoccupation with the paradox of justice and mercy is reflected in his deathbed letter to Roy and Alma Elliott (see Chapter I):

> How can we be just in a world that needs mercy and merciful in a world that needs justice.

This unsolved riddle—given no question mark in the letter—had wide-ranging social, political, and inevitably theological implications. It reached down to the mundane business of "Marking students in a kind of mockery and laughing it off." It had disturbing consequences for public welfare; Frost's innate independence balked at collectivist mass-mercy ("A Roadside Stand"):

> all these pitiful kin
> Are to be bought out and mercifully gathered in
> To live in villages next to the theater and store
> Where they won't have to think for themselves anymore;

It induced religious cynicism (*A Masque of Mercy*):

> The Sermon on the Mount
> Is just a frame-up to insure the failure
> Of all of us, so all of us will be
> Thrown prostrate at the Mercy Seat for Mercy.

Conversely, it inspired religious sympathy: " . . . how Christ posed Himself the whole problem and died for it" (letter to the Elliotts).

The graver aspects of mercy probably had not much touched Frost in the early twenties when he rejected the typescript title of the poem he soon called "Dust of Snow." But by the decade of the forties, the period of his two masques, the matter had become intensely personal and complex. Paul, in *A Masque of Mercy*, poses one aspect of the mercy-justice paradox:

> the most sacred thing of all's abruption.
> And if you've got to see your justice crossed
> (And you've got to) which will you prefer
> To see it, evil-crossed or mercy-crossed?

Frost's soul-searching in the forties was no doubt colored by a series of seemingly "evil-crossed" bereavements he had recently suffered—the death of his daughter Marjorie (a quite gifted poet) in 1934; his wife's sudden heart attack and death in 1938; his only surviving son Carol's suicide in 1940. The beneficent notion of unearned grace—the dust-of-snow type "mercy"—had, he learned, a grotesque underside: incomprehensible, undeserved, overwhelming tragedy. "There's no connection man can reason out/Between his just deserts and what he gets." So God tells Job in *A Masque of Reason*, and later adds, "the discipline man needed most/Was to learn his submission to unreason."

Some letters to friends at this time reveal the black depths to which Frost's spirits sank. To Louis Untermeyer he wrote in October 1940 after Carol's death:

> I took the wrong way with him. I tried many ways and every single one of them was wrong. Some thing in me is still asking for the chance to try one more. There's where the greatest pain is located.

The agonizing cry for another "chance" anticipates Keeper's plea for Jonah at the end of *A Masque of Mercy*. The theme of self-abasement in the masque (dramatized as an attempt to force Jonah's descent into Keeper's cellar, or *basement*) is forecast in another letter to Untermeyer, January 1942, containing an untitled poem that draws on Christian monasticism for its metaphor:

> To prayer I think I go,
> I go to prayer—
> Along a darkened corridor of woe
> And down a stair
> In every step of which I am abased.
> I wear a halter-rope about the waist.
> I bear a candle end put out with haste.
> For such as I there is reserved a crypt
> That from its stony arches having dripped
> Has stony pavement in a slime of mould.
> There I will throw me down an unconsoled
> And utter loss,
> And spread out in the figure of a cross.—

> Oh, if religion's not to be my fate
> I must be spoken to and told
> Before too late!

The letter itself is puzzling; referring to earlier versions of the poem, it concludes:

> You never saw how it came out. There was no end to it till now that I could write that I *had* been spoken to and told—you know by whom. . . . I believe I am safely secular till the last go down—that's all. I decided to keep the matter private and out of my new book. It could easily be made too much of. I can't myself say how serious the crisis was and how near I came to giving in.—It would have been good advertising.

Lawrance Thompson points out "the self-conscious ambivalence" between the poem and the comment in the letter, "I believe I am safely secular till the last go down." He reads "It" in the last line of the letter as "death" and sees in the poem a "sentimental fusion of suicide and crucifixion." But Thompson does not interpret the remark, "I *had* been spoken to and told—you know by whom." Unquestionably, we are left with an enigma and hints of some dire "crisis."

Besides such letters, a private notebook Frost kept during the forties registers his emotional state.[1] In a sequence of thoughts called "Dark Darker Darkest" he ponders unreasoning grief:

> Here where we are life wells up as a strong spring perpetually piling water on water with the dancing highlights fresh upon it. But it flows away on all sides as into a marsh of its own making. It flows away into poverty into insanity into crime. . . .

He attempts to rationalize sorrow, as a grim fruition of mortal striving, and he views poetry as a balm:

> . . . There is a residue of extreme sorrow that nothing can be done about and over it poetry lingers to brood with sympathy. I have heard poetry charged with having a vested interest in sorrow. Dark darker darkest. Dark as it is that there are these sorrows and darker still that we can do so little to get rid of them the darkest is still to

come. The darkest is that perhaps we ought not to want to get rid of them. They may be the fullfilment of exertion.

The entry continues by way of analogy:

What life craves most is signs of life. A cat can entertain itself only briefly with a block of wood. It can deceive itself longer with a spool or a ball. But give it a mouse for consummation. Response response The certainty of a source outside of self-original response whether love or hate fierceness or fear.

After two blank pages, he asks testily:

Why should we be the ones who had to apologize for our existance [sic] to the God who imposed it on us. I'm always being tried for heresy.

The masques, which Frost regarded as the culmination of his poetic achievement, between them embody two sides of a spiritual struggle. The Job-like rebellion of "Dark Darker Darkest" is reflected primarily in *A Masque of Reason* (1945), while *A Masque of Mercy* (1947) offers a kind of reconciliation—the seeds of which are planted in another "essay" in the notebook: "The Noblest Temptation. (God the Seducer.)" He invokes the gambling metaphor to illustrate the mystery of the Sermon on the Mount:

God too is out to win. He has made sure of the defeat of all who cant keep from reading the Sermon on the Mount. Many have found it irresistable [sic] reading. Commitment on commitment but none ever deliberate. Only as we are seduced can we be sure of our sincerity. Seduced into poetry—into marriage—into war° Into any form of art or society. . . . God breaks us on his Sermon, then gives us Heaven if we own up broken.

The idea is expanded in a note below:

°Into looking on the Sermon to be tempted by it to our surrender. The noblest the most beautiful temptation This is where time is requisite—a length of time however short for the trial to be set, the loss to be conceded, and the mercy to be brought on.

Then follows the curiously orthodox "Doctrine of Excursions," a blend of mild cynicism and humility:

> Out from God into a separateness affording him opposition and so back by defeat forgiveness and mercy into oneness with him again. The satisfaction must be all His (In one view The Sermon makes the game like the one at Monte Carlo all in favor of the house. [)]

The fixed "game" figure proceeds:

> God rigs it in a few loftiest councils so he takes all but intending always to give us more than our own back. It is like the greatest jest, but I can find no record or sign of God's having ever laughed any where. Comedy is pagan. The solemn hush of tragedy at the end is the beauty of Christianity.

He directly anticipates the second masque:

> God seems first to have become self conscious in his mercy in the book of Jonah. He thought it all out and exploited it to the full in the New Testament. Christ sacrificed himself rather to show us that we must sacrifice ourselves on the altar of his impossible ideals than to suffer vicariously to save us from sacrifice. No atonement/ quite vicarious.

Observing that "The Old Testament knew the vanity of vanities," Frost concludes the passage by rejecting the concept of justice:

> Justice is a very superficial consideration. We strive in the lists, we are seduce[d] into striving but the best we are often goes down[.] Job established it that there was no necessary connection between virtue and success or even ability and success. To the most we can achieve we shall say Vanity of Vanities. How much more is a king than a peasant. A pope than a pauper. Before these hard words of the Sermon we are all equally nobodies. The sin of seeking our own advantage that we were seduced into! That alone is enough to destroy us beyond ordinary forgiveness.

Frost liked to quote his rabbi friend Victor Reichert that Judaism and Christianity both "study the same book. . . . that all the material in the New [Testament] can be found in the Old."[2] Similarly, the masques are complementary, juxtaposing the God-of-Judgment and the God-of-Mercy. Frost called himself, ambiguously, "an Old Testament Christian." His "approach to Christ" was, like Keeper's, "more through Palestine" than "through Rome," and he would "rather be lost in the woods/Than found in church." "I don't go to church," he once quipped, "but I look in the window."[3] In the forties decade he looked in the window a good deal. The notebook records spiritual tensions that are subsumed in the dramatic format of the masques. In them, the cynicism and rebellion of the notebook jottings are voiced through a petulant Job and a skeptical Keeper; while Paul, discounting human vanity, speaks for the attitude of humility:

> Mercy is only to the undeserving.
> But such we all are made in the sight of God.
>
> "Oh, what is a king here,
> And what is a boor?
> Here all starve together.
> All dwarfed and poor."
>
> Here we all fail together, dwarfed and poor.
> Failure is failure, but success is failure.
> There is no better way of having it.

In *A Masque of Reason* God, on stage in the afterworld, is apt to sound smug in His omniscience: "a thousand years" before—during Job's earthly ordeal—God stacked the deck in His own favor. However, in *A Masque of Mercy* the sense of spiritual crisis is more acute. God is off stage but ever-present, in varying guises, in the minds and speech of the characters. He is the formidable Jehovah relentlessly pursuing Jonah; He represents the impossible Christian ideal that Keeper would prefer to disregard. The opening scene brings into focus the conflict between justice and mercy. The setting is a bookstore that has just closed for the night with one customer, Paul, locked inside. When the Fugitive (subsequently to be identified as Jonah) violently tries the door seeking asylum, the owner of the bookstore, Keeper, objects: "This is a bookstore—not a sanctuary." Keeper's wife, Jesse Bel, intercedes: "I thought you just now said it was a gift shop."

This exchange obliquely pinpoints the theological problem of the drama, the inadequacy of man's intellectual resources, alone, to achieve salvation. A "bookstore" is a place where one can acquire knowledge. But human knowledge, however vast one's book-learning, is at best limited. On the other hand, a "gift shop," by metaphoric extension, is a place where acquired knowledge and human merit are not at issue. The theme of the masque, the paradox of justice and mercy, is implicit in these alternatives. If what Keeper calls a "bookstore" is in fact a "gift shop," it may be a "sanctuary"—where safety, salvation even, is given to the undeserving.

Earlier, before Jesse Bel injects the notion of a gift shop, she has joined the others in attempting to refuse Jonah entrance: "We can't be always selling people things." His subsequent admittance suggests that sanctuary is not a commodity for barter. However, the dual function of the establishment metaphorically embodies the concepts both of justice—which the rational intellect finds comprehensible, and of mercy—which seems logically to contradict the principle of justice. To man's mind justice seems a fair trade; mercy, an unfair one. As Paul, New Testament spokesman, explains, "Mercy is only to the undeserving."

To establish his historic credentials, the Fugitive Jonah requests a Bible; but, ironically, Keeper, named by his idealistic mother for "My Brother's Keeper," permits no Bible in the store: people use it too often "To find out how to get away from God." Jonah, it develops, has run away from a speaking engagement in a hired hall where he was supposed to prophesy the doom of a wicked city (New York). "God's after me!" he exclaims. Remembering from his Biblical role the unfortunate experience of his "empty threat," he "shrink[s] from being publicly let down":

> I've lost my faith in God to carry out
> The threats He makes against the city evil.
> I can't trust God to be unmerciful.

Ostensibly, the drama is concerned with Jonah's plight and Paul's attempt to convert him to the view that *not* to trust God to be unmerciful is "the beginning of all wisdom." However, the real conversion takes place in the heart of the skeptic Keeper, who is gradually drawn toward the "lofty beauty" of the Sermon on the Mount, which he calls "An irresistible impossibility" that "no one can live up to/Yet no one turn from trying to live up to." But despite the Sermon's attraction for him, he resists:

> I won't deceive myself about success
> By making failure out of equal value.
> Any equality they may exhibit's
> In making fools of people equally.

It is Jonah's death that in the end causes Keeper to abandon his cynical resistance and to argue for Paul's point of view. The final lines of the masque are Keeper's, pleading for mercy—for Jonah and himself:

> And if I say we lift him from the floor
> And lay him where you ordered him to lie
> Before the cross, it is from fellow feeling,
> As if I asked for one more chance myself
> To learn to say (*He moves to Jonah's feet*)
> Nothing can make injustice just but mercy.

The last line of the drama resolves what Paul had earlier defined as God's "mercy-justice contradiction." To prostrate oneself before the cellar crucifix ("painted," we recall, "By a religious Aztec Indian") is to accept the religious paradox and be saved.

If Keeper's penchant for rationality makes him a "stubborn" convert, Jonah's passion for justice is a comparable obstacle. Paul commands him to descend to the cellar, through a doorway that stands open, to "Contemplate Truth until it burns [his] eyes out." Jonah does not "see any staircase," although Keeper assures him "There are stairs." Symbolically, Jonah wants step-by-step logic; he is unwilling to make the leap of faith:

> if winning ranks
> The same with God as losing, how explain
> Our making all this effort mortals make?

"Some lingering objection," Paul perceives, "holds [him] back." Jonah steps on the sill—the threshold of conversion, but the cellar door slams in his face; the blow crumples him to the floor, and he dies with Keeper and Paul kneeling beside him.

As Jesse Bel interprets the slammed door, Jonah is "rejected for his reservations." This use of *reservations* adds another dimension to the multivalent concept of *reserve*. We saw in Chapter II that reserve includes the affirmative rights of artistic privacy and divine secrecy. In *A Masque of Mercy* the connotation is negative; Jonah's "reservations" jeopardize his chance for eternal salvation. The masque implicitly raises a question that may be asked of Frost's own religious belief: Is there a clear-cut dividing line between being *noncommittal* and being *uncommitted*? I believe the two attitudes are separable, and that a failure among some critics to recognize this distinction has led to a misunderstanding of the place of religion in Frost's mind and work. The appropriate question is whether his reservations in matters of faith arise from being uncommitted, or merely noncommittal.

The difference between these attitudes is inherent in Keeper's remarks on "uncertainty":

> I can see that the uncertainty
> In which we act is a severity,
> A cruelty, amounting to injustice
> That nothing but God's mercy can assuage.

The lines maintain a perfect ambiguity. They may mean that man's uncertainty in action constitutes a severe, cruel, unjust affront to God, to be assuaged only by His mercy. Or, that God's imposing on man a condition of uncertainty, in which he must act, amounts to severe and cruel injustice, made bearable for man by God's mercy alone. The meanings do not cancel one another out; they serve to intensify the complexity of the man-God relationship. However interpreted, Keeper's concern is clearly with uncertainty in *action*. The need for courage to act, despite our uncertainty, is voiced at the end of the masque, in Keeper's prayer. He acknowledges his own "failure"—a failure of "courage"—as "no different from Jonah's":

> We both have lacked the courage in the heart
> To overcome the fear within the soul

And go ahead to any accomplishment.
Courage is what it takes and takes the more of
Because the deeper fear is so eternal.

The "deeper fear," as Paul explains it, is "the Fear of God"—
"Of God's decision lastly on your deeds." (The phrase echoes Mil-
ton's "Lycidas," which, according to Sidney Cox, Frost could re-
cite by heart.) Keeper, agreeing with Paul, differentiates this fear
from "the fear of punishment for sin"; he rejects possible reprisal
as a deterrent to wrong-doing. The "Fear of God" demands, according to Paul, not minimal virtue, but the very highest and best
of our efforts:

We have to stay afraid deep in our souls
Our sacrifice, the best we have to offer,
And not our worst nor second best, our best,
Our very best, our lives laid down like Jonah's,
Our lives laid down in war and peace, may not
Be found acceptable in Heaven's sight.
And that they may be is the only prayer
Worth praying.

Even when we have done our best, it is finally upon God's mercy,
not upon His justice alone, that salvation depends, for "Nothing
can make injustice just but mercy."

To see Keeper's conversion as Frost's own would be mistaken.
The masques are not testimonials to religious faith; they are the
fruit of spiritual struggle. Actually Keeper, more than any other
character, embodies the dual impulses—toward skepticism and
toward acceptance—in Frost himself. In a letter to Lawrance
Thompson in 1948 Frost emphasizes his own uneven spiritual
heritage:

You seem to reason that because my mother was religious, I must
have been religious too at any rate to start with. You might just as
well reason that because my father was irreligious I must have been
irreligious too.

The letter, of course, is calculated to frustrate his biographer's
desire to arrive at any conclusions as to the poet's religious belief.

Similarly, the spiritual probing which inspires the masques is shielded by protective levity. At heart the masques are not irreverent; they are "jokes" only in the sense of turn-about-is-fair-play, as a later couplet suggests:

> Forgive, O Lord, my little jokes on Thee
> And I'll forgive Thy great big one on me.

It is the power of forgiveness, of mercy, to offset the retributive justice of joking, but spiritual high jinks nevertheless have their place. In the masques they provide a way of accepting paradox with good humor, not straining after "wisdom that can have no counterwisdom."

V

An Acceptable Sacrifice

May my sacrifice
Be found acceptable in Heaven's sight.

—A MASQUE OF MERCY

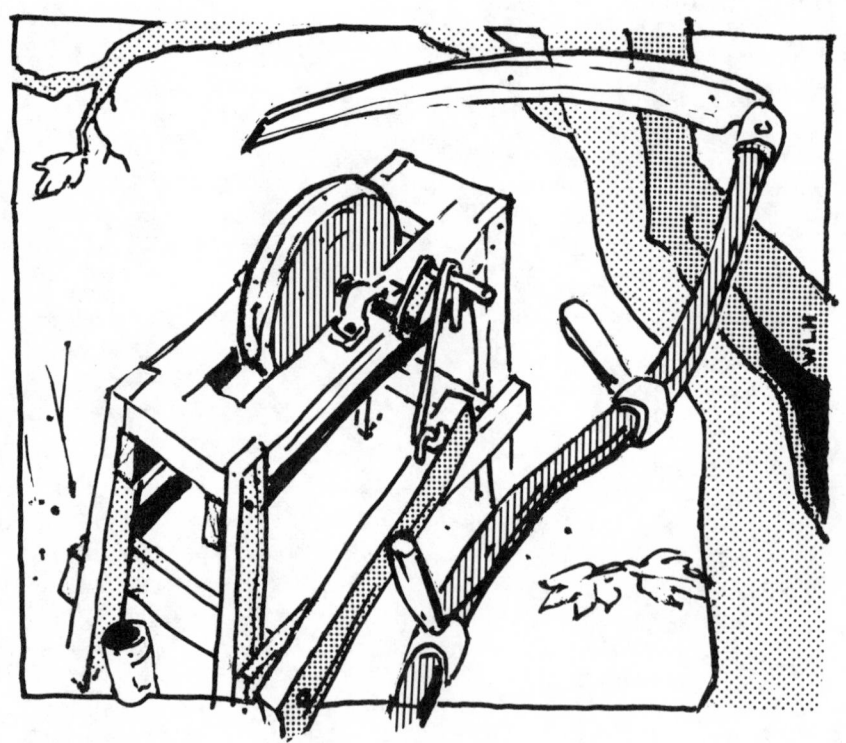

"THE GRINDSTONE"

Paul's prayer about the acceptability of his sacrifice recurs, little disguised, elsewhere in Frost during the decade of the masques. In 1947, writing Roy Elliott an apology for not planning to spend more time with him and his wife Alma on a coming visit to Amherst, he speculates on "blame" and deeper thoughts:

> I'm touching in Amherst only for four nights this time—I have decreed it and it cannot be otherwise. I can remember the time when I would have made the cowardly excuse that someone else wouldnt let me stay longer. Two world wars and a few private catastrophes have made a man of me who doesn't mind blame. . . . My fear of God has settled down into a deep inward fear that my best offering may not prove acceptable in his sight. I'll tell you most about it in another world. My approach to the New Testament is rather through Jerewsalem [sic] than through Rome and Canterbury.

Keeper's voice (his "approach to Christ"), as well as Paul's, is heard in the letter. Frost's remarks presumably fit into a long sequence of confidences; other correspondence with Elliott—especially Frost's deathbed letter—makes it clear that the two had delved much into spiritual matters.

Another letter, to Lawrance Thompson in the following year, associates the concept of *an acceptable sacrifice* explicitly with Frost's own poetic talent. The letter is peppered with skittishness and wit:

> I never prayed except formally and politely with the Lord's prayer in public. I used to try to get up plausible theories about prayer like Emerson. My latest is that it might be an expression of the hope I have that my offering of verse on the altar may be acceptable in His sight Whoever He is. Tell them I Am, Jehovah said. And as you know I have taken that as a command to iamb and not write free verse. It would be terribly dangerous to make too much of all this.

Frost toys with the notion of writing poetry as a religious vocation, then runs for the cover of a pun and summarily dismisses the topic.

The circumstances of writing the letter are amusing. It was a gratuitous response to some questions that Thompson, in the previous summer, didn't find the chance to ask—though he had written them down as surreptitious notes to himself. A rain shower had intervened on one of their walks in Ripton, Vermont, as Frost put it in the letter, "to save me from telling you lies." Frost discovered the questions "in your typewriting" (he declared accusingly) in a wool shirt left behind in the farmhouse the Thompsons rented from him for several summers. He left his belated reply, Thompson noted, "conspicuously propped against a sugar bowl on the dining table."

What the letter *avoids* saying about religious belief is fraught with more possibilities than what it says. It deals glancing blows at the central issue and repeatedly veers off into anecdote and fooling. When cornered by Frost for a verbal reaction to the letter, Thompson diplomatically replied that while it "hewed consistently to a solid line of argument, some of the chips that flew seemed more interesting than the line itself." To this, Thompson records, "RF . . . nodded as he winked one eye, and said quite sympathetically, 'Don't let me throw any dust in your eyes.' Then he changed the subject."

This exchange shows Frost maneuvering, as usual, for both communication and privacy. He might have pretended he never found Thompson's list of questions and averted an incident. But he couldn't resist springing the trap; he was out for some fun. Toward the middle of the letter he teases, "I grow curious about my soul out of sympathy for you in your quest for it. As you pronounce lastly on it of so much place in in [*sic*] Heaven I expect my reward." Leading then through a maze of banter and denial ("I'm afraid I stay a semidetached villain. But only semi,") he arrives at the tender confidence, "But I can leave it to you to give me a soul if you can. I know you will do your best for me."

Earlier, in 1946, Frost had spoken more seriously of "acceptable . . . offerings"—in a "sermon" he delivered in Cincinnati at the temple of his friend Rabbi Reichert:

> . . . the fear of God always has meant the fear that one's wisdom, one's own wisdom, one's own human wisdom is not quite acceptable in His sight. Always I hear that word 'acceptable'—'acceptable' about offerings like *that*, like offerings of mine. Always the fear that

it may not quite be acceptable. That, I take it, is the fear of God, and is with every religious nature, always.

The reluctance to second-guess God is analogous to Keeper's hesitation in *A Masque of Mercy*:

> But I'm too much afraid of God to claim
> I have been fighting on the angels' side.
> That is for Him and not for me to say.
> For me to say it would be irreligious.

It happened that on this trip to the Midwest Frost was carrying, for a reading (presumably at the University of Cincinnati, his sponsor), the unpublished manuscript of the masque. According to Lawrance Thompson, the poet later told Reichert that the service that First Day of the Feast of Tabernacles had helped him find precisely the ending he wanted for the masque. He wrote Reichert in 1953 and asked him to supply the words of a vaguely remembered prayer about "sacrifice," calling it "the heart and center of all religion." "It is kindred in spirit," he said, "to 'Nevertheless not my will but Thy will.'" The rabbi referred him to Psalm 19, verse 14:

> Let the words of my mouth, and the meditation of my heart be acceptable before Thee, O Lord, my Rock, and my Redeemer.

The phrase "offerings of mine" in the "sermon" is, no doubt, related to "my offering of verse on the altar" in the "sugar-bowl" letter of 1948. Why, we may ask, did Frost incline to the view that the role of poet is a sacred calling?

A clue is lodged in an open letter he wrote to *The Amherst Student* of 1935, in which he draws, probably unconsciously, upon the thought of Henri Bergson. But the roots of Bergsonian influence reach back to 1911 when Frost first read the American translation of *Creative Evolution*. While his initial fascination with Bergson eventually subsided, Frost's thinking received an indelible, if indistinct, mark from the French philosopher—especially discernible in the material and spiritual confluences of "West-Running Brook." Frost turned to Bergson, as he had earlier—in his

Harvard days—to William James, to buttress what he called his "freethinker" tendencies. These two provided a way of maintaining a healthy skepticism toward the rigidity of orthodox Christian belief—a way consistent with private spiritual faith. Bergson furnished also a means of endowing the theories of material evolutionists with spiritual meanings—of linking the intuitive consciousness of the artist to the *élan vital* of the universal creative process.

Bergson's universe was not a finished product but "a perpetual growth, a creation pursued without end." "Every human work," according to Bergson, "in which there is invention . . . brings something new into the world." Through the form-making power of the imagination "the universe . . . is being made continually. It is growing, perhaps indefinitely, by the addition of new worlds."

The concept of an ongoing creative process in which man, the highest creature, collaborates with a vital force, furnished Frost with a moral ground for artistic form-making. His letter to *The Amherst Student* recognizes the etymological root of the word *poet* (*maker*):

> There is at least so much good in the world that it admits of form and the making of form. And not only admits of it, but calls for it. We people are thrust forward out of the suggestions of form in the rolling clouds of nature. In us nature reaches its height of form and through us exceeds itself. When in doubt there is always form for us to go on with. Anyone who has achieved the least form to be sure of it, is lost to the larger excruciations. I think it must stroke faith the right way. The artist [,] the poet [,] might be expected to be the most aware of such assurance. But it is really everybody's sanity to feel it and live by it.

The use of *sanity* obliquely acknowledges the therapeutic side-effect of form-making in every walk of life. Recall the pleasure Silas, the hired man, found in his "one accomplishment," bundling hay, "every forkful in its place,/ . . . tag[ged] and number[ed]." Frost once quipped, "There's nothing so composing as composition." *The Amherst Student* letter goes further; it invests the personal gratification of form-making with cosmic significance. It sees the activity even as conducive to "faith." The design of the universe—from the nebulous "suggestions of form in the rolling clouds of nature" to the "height of form" in human nature—not only "admits of" creative composition, but "calls for it." Such a universe is, however minimally, moral, not amoral; its form-making potential is suggestive of "at least" a margin of "good." And man, as maker-of-form, must be an instrument in a natural scheme. He must be the vehicle through whom cosmic design reaches toward highest expression.

"Design," Lawrance Thompson wrote me once, "is a sacred word to [Frost], and he's being tricky in his poem entitled 'Design' " (I had spoken of its "if-y" conclusion).[1] His letter points specifically to this passage in *The Amherst Student* where design is a factor in personal salvation:

> One can safely say after from six to thirty thousand years of experience that the evident design is a situation here in which it will always be about equally hard to save your soul. Whatever progress may be taken to mean, it can't mean making the world any easier a place in which to save your soul—or if you dislike hearing your soul mentioned in open meeting, say your decency, your integrity.

In Frost's strategic retreat from the unabashedly theological "soul" to the ostensibly secular "integrity," he returns to root-meaning: "wholeness of being," with all the religious implications that "wholeness" had for him. As for worldly progress, he regarded it as questionable; the notion of earth as perpetual trial-ground of the soul persisted from his days in Lawrence High School. "The Lesson for Today" finds all ages, over the millennia, about equally "dark." His response, however, is not despair, but action. "There is something," *The Amherst Student* letter asserts, "we can always be doing without reference to how good or how bad the age is." The "something" is the making-of-form—for Frost himself, the making-of-poems.

His dedication to form, to design, was total though his demand upon it was modest. He wrote to Sidney Cox in 1929:

> A little in the fist to manipulate is all I ask. My object is true form—
> is was and always will be—form true to any chance bit of true life.
> Almost any bit will do. I dont naturally trust any other object.

He was then, as always, adhering to the principle of synecdoche—
an ordered universe implicit in any odd scraps of form. Truth-to-
life was his criterion. He once told some Bread Loaf listeners he
disliked "gilting gold, when a thing is pretty in itself"; "I'd rather
have it strong." "Poetry is gloating on facts," he said of "Mowing,"
calling it "one of my earliest poems and convictions":

> Anything more than the truth would have seemed too weak
> To the earnest love that laid the swale in rows.

To strive for more than bare truth, to embellish or adorn it, is to
weaken it. "A poet," Frost believed, "must lean hard on facts, so
hard, sometimes, that they hurt."[2] He relished "crudity," by which
he meant "rawness," "raw material," "the part of life not yet
worked up into form, or at least not worked all the way up." "A
real artist delights in roughness for what he can do to it." He
pointed out the utopian "fallacy" of "pin[ing] for a life that shall
be nothing but finished art."[3] Art, like the life it reflects, must have
some unhoned roughness. He admired Shakespeare's "slap-dash"
genius. "The only great art is inesthetic . . . ."

The delicate balance in art between roughness and polished
form is a basic theme in "The Grindstone." The poem asks the
tantalizing aesthetic question, in its own metaphor: When is a
"blade" ground fine enough? By extension, it raises more baffling
moral issues: When is any human endeavor the best it can be? Can
man attain perfection? Should he try? Why does all mortal effort
involve suffering and sacrifice? When is the work of man's hands
acceptable in terms of the highest reach of his talent?

Mythic in scope, "The Grindstone" seeks to bring into align-
ment the Bergsonian theory of evolution and the Biblical story of
the Fall. Man's role as form-maker, in a universe continually
evolving—yet forever imperfect—is juxtaposed with his deadly
legacy from Adam of sin and suffering. Technically difficult, the
poem is as obstinate in yielding meaning as the cantankerous
grindstone is in granting satisfaction to the man who cranks it. Yet
sparks fly off at odd angles as the poem laboriously grinds along:
ideas about time and so-called progress, about creativity, about
discord and destruction, about human striving and sacrifice.

The basic metaphor draws upon the grindstone theory of the universe; the grindstone is intended as an analogue for the world. The poem gets off to a deliberately "cumbersome" start, backing into its subject by way of gerund phrase and circumlocution. Irregular rhyme and rhythm lend an added sense of roughness:

> Having a wheel and four legs of its own
> Has never availed the cumbersome grindstone
> To get it anywhere that I can see.
> These hands have helped it go, and even race;
> Not all the motion, though, they ever lent,
> Not all the miles it may have thought it went,
> Have got it one step from the starting place.
> It stands beside the same old apple tree.

Not all wheel-spinning, the lines suggest, can be called progress. John F. Lynen observes that the colloquialism " 'To get somewhere' connotes a kind of movement that is less efficient and purposeful than 'to go' or 'to travel.' It implies clumsiness, great efforts for small results . . . ."[4] Farther on, the poem again cynically comments:

> I wondered what machine of ages gone
> This represented an improvement on.
> For all I knew it may have sharpened spears
> And arrowheads itself.

The stubborn grindstone, "worn" by usage to "an oblate/Spheroid [like the planet earth] that kicked and struggled in its gait," had been rendered less efficient through the passage of time than its ancient predecessor which had "sharpened spears/And arrowheads." If "improvement" is measured as scientific advance from primitive weapons to devices more sophisticated and devastating, then so-called progress is a fallacy. As in *The Amherst Student* letter, a denial of worldly progress is linked, by implication here, to human suffering:

> I gave it the preliminary spin,
> And poured on water (tears it might have been),

The mythic context of man's burden of sorrow is suggested by the location of the grindstone: "It stands beside the same old apple tree." The shade from the tree—like the darkness cast from the Garden of Eden—falls upon the grindstone as it turns season after season:

> The shadow of the apple tree is thin
> Upon it now, its feet are fast in snow.

In the late world of winter the grindstone is still "standing in the yard/Under a ruinous live apple tree." The conjunction of thought in "ruinous live" is provocative; though "ruinous"—full of rot—the tree survives, a living emblem of decay and mortality. The blight infecting the tree spreads ruin to things under its apparently protective, potentially pernicious "shadow."

Stylistically intricate, the poem is also ponderous in overall structure. Frost abandons his more familiar dramatic beginning (the initial "I" that launches directly into action). The opening stanza—twenty-five lines—does little but set the scene for the drama of the second. Moreover that action is distanced, introduced as a glimpse of a summer long ago. Some vague sense of Adam's Fall seems to jar memory, as if by associative guilt; the man tries to deny any significance (for him) of the grindstone:

> its standing in the yard
> Under a ruinous live apple tree
> Has nothing any more to do with me,
> Except that I remember how of old
> One summer day, all day I drove it hard,
> And someone mounted on it rode it hard,
> And he and I between us ground a blade.

His denial is refuted by a haunting reminiscence that crowds in upon his consciousness and spills forth, in stanza two, remote and dream-like—a kind of ancestral reverie from some primeval time. The nameless "someone" emerges as a mysterious "Father-Time" figure who peers "funny-eyed" over "spectacles that glowed." Symbol of human mortality, he is a natural antagonist to the man driving the wheel. It is a questionable cooperative venture, for the design of the grindstone requires that the two men work at odds. The harder the one presses the blade against the wheel, the more slowly it turns, and the more arduous becomes the other's cranking. The turning grindstone, like the earth in its rotation, exacts a toll upon the flesh. The time a man *spends* on a task *expends* his energy, bringing him closer to death. (The inherent opposition of life and time is noted also in "West-Running Brook": "Our life runs down in sending up the clock.") In a grindstone-like universe human suffering and sacrifice are built-in features of the operation; time, not man, has the last word:

> I wondered who it was the man thought ground—
> The one who held the wheel back or the one
> Who gave his life to keep it going round?
> I wondered if he really thought it fair
> For him to have the say when we were done.
> Such were the bitter thoughts to which I turned.

There is further irony in this drama of grinding: not only must the two men, in performing a job both want to complete, work against each other, but their objective is of doubtful merit. They are sharpening the blade of Time's "scythe," symbolic instrument of human destruction. A moral cloud hangs over their endeavor; the end-product can be used for either good or evil. (Time's being "Armed" suggests *his* malicious intent.) A scythe, like any other blade, is a tool or a weapon depending on the vantage point. It may help a man to maintain a farm, but it may also be turned against him; to the living grass, of course, the scythe is a weapon. (In "The Objection to Being Stepped On," a humorous reversal of swords-into-ploughshares, "an unemployed hoe" delivers a sharp crack to the head.)

Good and evil throughout "The Grindstone" are inextricably intertwined. So also are harmony and discord, creativity and destruction. Two antagonists "pass the afternoon/ . . . grinding discord out of a grindstone" to make a blade perfect. Looked at one way, the "gritty tune" of their grinding tends toward a creative, harmonious goal. The finer the blade becomes, the less rau-

cous will be the "tune." But from another perspective their aim is
destructive, for to grind a finer blade is to produce a sharper,
more lethal weapon.

Such a network of moral ambiguities leaves finally unrecon-
ciled Bergsonian theory and Biblical myth. If creative evolution
tends optimistically toward ever higher levels of cosmic order,
the story of the Fall adds a darker dimension, taking into account
the existence of evil, suffering, and destruction. In the last stanza,
the moral center of the poem, the philosophic emphasis is distinctly Biblical rather than Bergsonian. Here it develops that their
labor is ultimately futile. They strive for an unfeasible ideal, like
the "irresistible impossibility" of the Sermon on the Mount that
Keeper says "no one can live up to." Without knowing, the grind-
ers may be "only wasting precious blade"; error in human judgment always stands between man and the abstract goal of *fine-
ness*. Not only is perfection beyond man's grasp, but to strive to
attain it is, in religious terms, to usurp divinity—like Adam, to
pluck the forbidden fruit:

> Wasn't there danger of a turn too much?
> Mightn't we make it worse instead of better?
> I was for leaving something to the whetter.
> What if it wasn't all it should be? I'd
> Be satisfied if he'd be satisfied.

"Disinterestedly," the figure of Time grinds on; the other, sens-
ing the imperfection of their machine, all but cries out in fear. He
knows that only a hand-held whetstone, not the coarser grindstone, can hone to a finer polish, and he is "satisfied" to leave their
present edge well enough alone.

Is "the whetter" a reference to some final judge of mortal
effort—to God? We can only guess. Frost's well-used phrase "unfinished business"—he said it with amused resignation—comes to
my mind when I read the end of "The Grindstone." So, too, does
the final line of "Good-By and Keep Cold" where in winter the
apple orchard "sinks lower under the sod":

> But something has to be left to God.

I think of that other Eden-myth poem (see page 3), and the sense
of drowsy fulfillment in an uncompleted task:

> there may be two or three
> Apples I didn't pick upon some bough.
> But I am done with apple-picking now.

And of "Unharvested," where nature compensates for human
negligence. "An apple fall/As complete as the apple had given
man," from a tree pickers have overlooked, paints the ground beneath "one circle of solid red":

> May something go always unharvested!
> May much stay out of our stated plan,
> Apples or something forgotten and left,
> So smelling their sweetness would be no theft.

Restraint (such as Adam and Eve in their "theft" abused) may
yield unexpected benefits. I think finally of "The Wood-Pile"
where nature picks up and completes a woodcutter's abandoned
chore; "a cord of maple," left "far from a useful fireplace,"
"warm[ed] the frozen swamp as best it could/With the slow
smokeless burning of decay":

> I thought that only
> Someone who lived in turning to fresh tasks
> Could so forget his handiwork on which
> He spent himself, the labor of his ax, . . .

Like "The Grindstone," these poems recognize human frailty and
imply trust that somehow man's deficiencies may be offset, may
be found acceptable.

VI

The Holiness of Wholeness

So by craft or art
We can give the part
Wholeness in a sense.

—"KITTY HAWK"

"KITTY HAWK"

"I can't write of a grief in a grief. I have to wait," Frost told an interviewer in 1962, "but sometimes a poem has saved me." To Frost poetry was no substitute for the analyst's couch; he did not belong to the "confessional" school. The configurations of grief took time to emerge:

> Let chaos storm!
> Let cloud shapes swarm!
> I wait for form.

As an artist, Frost relied on his craft for getting in touch with psychic needs, for giving order to overwhelming sorrows—however modestly he might state his case, however tamed such emotions might seem, transformed into poetry. But when Frost spoke of the "saving" power of poetry, was he thinking of it as an elevated, intellectualized kind of basket-weaving, as psychic therapy in the clinical sense of emotional and mental adjustment to the pressures of life? Or did salvation-through-poetry mean something more comprehensive?

There are hints, as we find in his letter to *The Amherst Student*, that Frost linked poetry to "salvation" in its religious meaning—a redeeming of the psyche or, by derivation, of the human soul. The hints are often tinged with coyness, couched in teasing, touched on so lightly that they may be missed altogether. He glances briefly, for example, at the day that was "saved" by a feather-dusting of snow ("Dust of Snow"), and we see no particular reason to search for theological implications. Or he makes sport, almost a mockery, of the idea of saving souls, writing to Roy Elliott (1938):

> I just wanted to be sure if you were going to use poetry for the salvation of souls you had counted the cost to poetry. But you deny in your letter that you ever had used poetry for the salvation of souls. Really it would be all right with me if you had. Use poetry or friendship or anything else you please to corner me for my soul's salvation. We are all each other's keepers.

Nevertheless there is evidence that Frost took seriously the spiritual impact of salvation-by-poetry. He liked to draw the cryptic inference from Saint Matthew and Saint Mark that "you can't be saved unless you have some poetry in you." If this sounds like joking, remember that the notion forms an underlying motif in one of his most difficult and thoughtful poems, "Directive."[1] More explicitly, he said at Amherst in 1931 ("Education by Poetry"):

> The only materialist—be he poet, teacher, scientist, politician, or statesman—is the man who gets lost in his material without a gathering metaphor to throw it into shape and order. He is the lost soul.

By "a gathering metaphor" Frost meant any figure of order that might be culled from the raw material of living, any random fragments of form, however accidental they may seem, that might give life a sense of purpose:

> Grant me intention, purpose, and design—
> That's near enough for me to the Divine.

These lines from "Accidentally on Purpose" might suggest that, in a world where *God is dead*, the arbitrary ordering of things furnishes a workable substitute for "the Divine." But I think they mean, quite literally, "near enough"—in the way that, figuratively, the ladder in "After Apple-Picking" points "*Toward* heaven," while set firmly on earth—or in the way that human love, in "A Prayer in Spring," is, in miniature, divine love. In Jamesian terms, we might say that the lines state the principle of *multum in parvo*, the demonstration of "much in little"—the grand design in the lesser. I read them as indicative of Frost's fondness for synecdoche; not just an aesthetic fondness, but one that shows his faith in the accessibility, through bits and pieces, of an ordered universe. *The Amherst Student* letter supports this view:

> To me any little form I assert upon [the background of black and utter chaos] is velvet, as the saying is, and to be considered for how much more it is than nothing. If I were a Platonist I should have to consider it, I suppose, for how much less it is than everything.

To gather metaphors is to ask for little and hope for much; it is aspiratory, a reach for "something like a star/To stay our minds on and be staid" ("Choose Something Like a Star")—even if the stay is only "momentary," as Frost says in "The Figure a Poem Makes." We remember the "Education by Poetry" talk (see pages 11-12) and his forceful description of "the height of all poetic thinking": an "attempt to say matter in terms of spirit, or spirit in terms of matter . . . the greatest attempt that ever failed." Yet metaphor, to him, was the zenith of intellectual ambition, like the fancied desire of fireflies to emulate stars in "Fireflies in the Garden":

> Here come real stars to fill the upper skies,
> And here on earth come emulating flies,
> That though they never equal stars in size,
> (And they were never really stars at heart)
> Achieve at times a very star-like start.
> Only, of course, they can't sustain the part.

Or, metaphor might be compared to the sparks rising from the sugarhouse chimney in "Evening in a Sugar Orchard":

> The sparks made no attempt to be the moon.
> They were content to figure in the trees
> As Leo, Orion, and the Pleiades.
> And that was what the boughs were full of soon.

In the phrase "They were content," the sparks display an inverse modesty; they make no claim to match the moon, only "to figure" (to make metaphor) as constellations of stars—which are in fact radiating sources of light, not mere reflectors like a moon.

Again, in "New Hampshire," the celestial "thrust" of metaphor is like an urge to reach higher still from mountain tops for something starlike:

> [I] cannot rest from planning day or night
> How high I'd thrust the peaks in summer snow
> To tap the upper sky and draw a flow
> Of frosty night air on the vale below
> Down from the stars to freeze the dew as starry.

All these images suggest a quest for "the final unity" of spirit and matter. The figure a poem or a life might make was achieved in striving toward this wholeness of being. To fail to strive was to become "the lost soul."

The philosophical basis for the quest of wholeness through a synecdochic approach to art, to living, crystallizes in a long poem from Frost's "post-late" period, "Kitty Hawk," a work Lawrance Thompson found "thematically central" to the poet's last book. About a year after the appearance of an early version in *The Atlantic Monthly*, November 1957, Frost had remarked:

> My theme is that the only *event* in all history is science plunging deeper into matter. We have plunged into the smallness of particles and we are plunging into the hugeness of space—but not without fears that the spirit shall be lost. . . . in taking us deeper and deeper into matter, science has left all of us with this great misgiving, this fear that we won't be able to substantiate the spirit.[2]

At that time he had contemplated the title *The Great Misgiving* for what came to be called *In the Clearing*, a fact that supports the centrality of "Kitty Hawk." The change of title implies a transition from uncertainty to affirmation, an establishing of clarity. But the "misgiving" in the poem remains. It arises from the presence, the absolute necessity, of risk:

> Someone asked me if I thought God *could* take a chance. I said it looked to me as if he had—right from the start.

In May 1958, in a copy of his *Complete Poems* which he gave to Father Arthur MacGillivray of Boston College, Frost penned six lines with a heading "The Risk." They were actually a fragment from "Kitty Hawk," and ended "the supreme merit/Lay in risking spirit/In substantiation." "Kitty Hawk" enlarges the notion of earth-as-trial-ground. Earth is a place where not only man, but God, too, is on trial. The poem views the Garden of Eden myth as a metaphor for the "chance" God took in creating man, a being free and fallible. It was a risk, a commitment of God's spirit to the material world. Adam's freedom to taste the fruit of the tree of knowledge symbolized the ongoing penetration of *man's* spirit into matter, and anticipated the quandary of the Occident:

> . . . only the Western world has really risked it. The people of the East had the great misgiving, but it arrested them. They drew back from the material because they weren't ready to take the dare of it.

The principal metaphor in "Kitty Hawk" is drawn from Genesis; the philosophical argument may appear partially Bergsonian, but it is basically Judeo-Christian. To Bergson, man's free consciousness was the single factor distinguishing him *in kind* "from the rest of the animal world"; by virtue of his free will, man is "the 'term' and the 'end' of evolution":

> . . . in the animal, invention is never anything but a variation on the theme of routine. . . . With man, consciousness breaks the chain. In man, and in man alone, it sets itself free.

Freedom is the driving force in Bergson's universe, a cosmos evolving by man's conscious invention. So also is human freedom fundamental in the world of "Kitty Hawk," "starring man/In the royal role." However, the decidedly moral concern of the poem grounds it ultimately in Biblical, rather than in Bergsonian, thought. *Creative Evolution* speaks of "God" (the *élan vital*) as "unceasing life, action, freedom"; it ignores the problem of evil, of human sin, that, Biblically, is essential to God's extending His freedom-of-action to man. "God" in "Kitty Hawk" is a risk-taker and the *morality* of man's use of his own freedom is a basic issue.

"Kitty Hawk" celebrates the flight of the Wrights' biplane, herald of the Space Age, as symbolic of the "venture" of Western civilization: " . . . one mighty charge/On our human part/Of the soul's ethereal/Into the material." Modern science—the word comes from the Latin *scire*, "to know"—is, after all, a perpetuation of Adam's thirst for knowledge. And the entire plunge of human consciousness into the material universe is an extension of God's initial thrust into corporeal being. The freedom to dare was the essence of the divine experiment, for man must be free to become lost in order for God to be free to save him:

> Pulpiteers will censure
> Our instinctive venture
> Into what they call
> The material
> When we took that fall
> From the apple tree.
> But God's own descent
> Into flesh was meant
> As a demonstration
> That the supreme merit
> Lay in risking spirit
> In substantiation.
> Westerners inherit
> A design for living
> Deeper into matter—
> Not without due patter
> Of a great misgiving.

"Substantiation" is a heavy-duty word; as Frost would say, it goes "for pay dirt." Signifying the entering of the spirit into material form, it suggests also an affirmation, a confirmation, of the spirit—a weighty responsibility. The "zest" of science "To materialize/By on-penetration/Into earth and skies" is both admirable and foolhardy, for the "spirit" may be lost in the process. The poem is ambivalent toward human knowledge, observing its power and promise, its perils and limits. It recommends a synecdochic approach to living:

> But the comfort is
> In the covenant
> We may get control
> If not of the whole
> Of at least some part
> Where not too immense,
> So by craft or art
> We can give the part
> Wholeness in a sense.

This sequence occurs in the next-to-last section of "Kitty

Hawk"; the title of the section, "The Holiness of Wholeness," carries the full import of what Frost intended by salvation-through-poetry. The title recognizes an inherent bond between psychic and spiritual integrity. The terms "Holiness" and "Wholeness," Frost knew, come from the same Anglo-Saxon root, and their conjunction implies that the sense of wholeness he sought in synecdoche embodies emotional, mental, and spiritual integration.

"Kitty Hawk" deals with risk in cosmic terms. Frost, in fact, saw the challenge to a poet as analogous to the one God posed for Himself. In "The Constant Symbol" he writes, "The bard has said in effect, Unto these forms did I commend the spirit." We might guess, from the scriptural tone, that writing a poem was to Frost an act of consecration. "It may take [a poet] a year after the act to confess he only betrayed the spirit with a rhymster's cleverness . . . ":

> Had he anything to be true to? Was he true to it? Did he use good words? You couldn't tell unless you made out what idea they were supposed to be good for. Every poem is an epitome of the great predicament; a figure of the will braving alien entanglements.

The poet's "predicament" is a constant symbol of mankind's universal "misgiving," and poetry therefore must be play-with-words "for mortal stakes" ("Two Tramps in Mud Time"). It is a play in which the "spirit" of a work of art is in continual danger of being distorted or even lost in the exigencies of meter, of rhyme, of language itself. Writing a poem is a commitment of the artist's inner self to the intransigencies of outer form:

> Every single poem written regular is a symbol small or great of the way the will has to pitch into commitments deeper and deeper to a rounded conclusion and then be judged for whether any original intention it had has been strongly spent or weakly lost. . . .

Artistic judgment is inseparable from moral judgment. "Strongly spent," Frost adds, "is synonymous with kept"—or, he might have said, with *saved*. The form he demanded in poetry was not merely verbal, not merely aesthetic; it was substantial, an embodiment that could substantiate the impulse that gave it birth. If earth is a testing-place, then a poet's *words* must be judged as "deeds":

> Sometimes I have my doubts of words altogether and I ask myself what is the place of them. They are worse than nothing unless they can do something, unless they amount to deeds as in ultimatums or battle-cries. They must be flat and final like the show-down in poker, from which there is no appeal. My definition of poetry (if I were forced to give one) would be this: words that have become deeds.[3]

"Kitty Hawk" might actually be considered an *article of belief*, perhaps the closest Frost came to declaring the potentially spiritual significance of human action—and, by implication, of a poet's "deeds." We find in "Kitty Hawk" an assertive rationale for Frost's synecdochic, or fragmentary, approach—an argument we may draw upon to respond to the charge that Frost's vision suffers from "incompleteness," that he lacks the comprehensive scope of, say, Dante or Yeats.[4] Such a judgment is accurate to the extent that his vision is incremental—continually evolving, as the universe itself evolves. In 1937 at Princeton University ("The Poet's Next of Kin in a College") he developed a metaphor to describe the process of maturing, one which we may apply to his own growth as artist. In his early poetry, words and images "flash here and . . . there . . . like the stars coming out in the . . . evening." "Later in the dark of life" we discern the emergence of "constellations"—patterns delineated by his language and imagery. Individual poems signal back and forth to each other across the years of his writing. Words group into clusters as tight as the Pleiades. They become variations upon a single, if complex, idea: favor-grace-mercy; wholeness-holiness; looking-watching-seeing. Like his "peaceful shepherd," turned astronomer, we "line the figures in" between his "dotted" images, and his night sky is illumined by metaphor.

If, as "Kitty Hawk" indicates, Frost attributed a measure of "holiness" to the act of gathering metaphors—if Lawrance Thompson is correct that "design is a sacred word to him"—then some disturbing questions arise about the implications of that bleak little poem he called "Design." Its symbolic logic, sonnet shape, and unusual rhyme scheme join to create bitter ironies, troubling ambiguities. A diagram is useful for examining the resonating patterns of sound:

I found a dimpled spider, fat and white,   a
On a white heal-all, holding up a moth   b
Like a white piece of rigid satin cloth—   b
Assorted characters of death and blight   a
Mixed ready to begin the morning right,   a
Like the ingredients of a witches' broth—   b
A snow-drop spider, a flower like a froth,   b
And dead wings carried like a paper kite.   a

What had that flower to do with being white,   a
The wayside blue and innocent heal-all?   c
What brought the kindred spider to that height,   a
Then steered the white moth thither in the night?   a
What but design of darkness to appall?—   c
If design govern in a thing so small.   c

3 quatrains (3 rhyme sounds) ———
6 (2×3) couplets (3 rhyme sounds) ———
2 tercets (2 rhyme sounds) ———

Fashioning this sonnet as basically Petrarchan in structure—with stanzaic division into octave and sestet—Frost departs from the conventions of that form as if to avoid predictability. We are accustomed, in the sonnets of Petrarch and his Italian followers, to have a problem propounded in the first eight lines, resolved in the final six. But the opening of "Design" merely *presents* a dramatic episode, leaving any inherent problem to inference. Traditionally, the octave may express indignation, desire, doubt—some heightened pitch of feeling; but here emotion is held in check. With an air of indifference, Frost sets before us a trinity "of death and blight": a pock-marked ("dimpled"), bloated ("fat"), colorless ("white") spider; a moth with *rigor-mortis* wings; an anemic mutation of the ordinarily curative blue herb, the "heal-all." A "mixed" assortment, they somehow blend together into a poisonous concoction, "a witches' broth." We wonder silently, as these "characters . . . begin the morning right," just what is the appropriateness (*right*ness) of their situation. Is there some obscure purpose in this apparently satanic ritual (*rite*)?

Not until the sestet does this sonnet—abruptly—give voice to its questions. Why is the normally "innocent" medicinal flower *itself* sick? What directive force, if any, "steered" the moth to its doom, at the hands of its kith-or-"kindred" spider? (By implication, what or who engineered this moribund plot?) The final two lines of the poem multiply the ironies, offering dual—and contradictory—explanations for a deadly tableau etched in palest white: either some malevolent power staged this dire interlude; or it happened at random, by pure chance. Could any order, though it may exist in the universe, affect such insignificant creatures? Or, if order is absent in this microcosm, then it is perhaps missing in the macrocosm, too.

As the diagram shows, the sestet breaks into *unmatched* tercets. Looked at another way, the poem ends with a couplet—a characteristic of the Elizabethan sonnet. Petrarch did not use a final couplet, although by 1540 some other Italian sonneteers were using it;[5] he took *six* lines to explore a solution to the issue(s) introduced in the octave. But English practitioners—Wyatt, Spenser, Shakespeare—altered the rhyme scheme and shifted the balance in the poetic argument by expanding their inquiry to twelve lines and laying it to rest in an epigrammatic *two*. The end of Frost's poem—with its vestigial Elizabethan couplet grafted onto a fundamentally Petrarchan stanza pattern—manages to dash our expectations once again. Looking for a stock answer, we are given only the darkest ambiguities, quasi-solutions that cancel one another: one poses a last *question*; the other is in the *conditional* mode ("If").

"Design" is a subvertive piece. (I'm borrowing from Frost himself—he called Emerson a "subvertive" thinker.) Its rhyme adheres to Petrarch in the octave, but departs from the Italian poet thereafter. The progression of its metaphoric argument also undermines strict Petrarchan form, by using (like the Elizabethans) a full twelve lines to state the problem. Then the closing couplet circumvents all hope of resolution and adds yet another dimension to the puzzle. Instead of the conventional sonnet formula, propound/resolve, the strategy appears to be: *propound/ confound.*[6]

The poem exhibits a multitude of *threes* in its design, and this *trinitarian* emphasis may, too, be subvertive, parodying Christian theology. With its cast of three actors (active and passive), it depends, through its fourteen lines, on just three rhymes (Italian sonnets generally have five), and it asks three explicit questions overall—though others are implied. Its more obvious stanza structure is octave/sestet, but concealed in this pattern are three quatrains, not all immediately consecutive, of similar rhyme scheme: abba abba caac. And there are six (twice three) couplets. The severe limitations in sound tend toward lyric stillness rather than toward the narrative progression of an Elizabethan sonnet. The hovering rhymes create an *auditory* compactness, as tight-knit as the *visual* scene the octave depicts. Three-ness is compressed toward one-ness, even if that unity be a total nullification of cosmic order. Utterly succinct, "Design" shatters metaphysical certitude as effectively as *Being and Nothingness*, Sartre's long philosophical treatise in which he faces *le néant* on the universal level, finding his way back to meaningful action on the human level. Frost, however—with that little "If"—gives himself, and us, the option of pervasive design or chaos. → I think it is design

We may object that the *first* alternative, carrying the heavy connotation of malice aforethought, is as unsavory as the *second*: anarchy everywhere. Moreover, from an artistic standpoint, why does this poem of "threes" offer only two tentative answers to its riddle? I think the "appall"-ing couplet, which seems to throw a *pall* upon the preceding lines, will admit of a third possibility, more hopeful. "A thing so small" can be not just the sinister *natural* event in the poem, but the poem itself, the *art* miniature which contains the event. If a sonnet can be made so nearly perfect, a thing of formal beauty, then what may be the potential for design on a larger scale, all-encompassing? This is a poem of exploration, not solution. Like Walt Whitman's "noiseless patient spider," Frost has "launch'd forth filament, filament, filament, . . . / Ever unreeling them." But the "gossamer thread" he spins does not "catch somewhere," does not form any "bridge" of affirmation. Instead, it traps us with its intriguing equivocations.

VII

All Revelation

Eyes seeking the response of eyes
Bring out the stars, bring out the flowers,
Thus concentrating earth and skies
So none need be afraid of size.
All revelation has been ours.

—"ALL REVELATION"

"ALL REVELATION"

Frost's "revelation" poems tempt us to religious conjecture. He regarded poetry itself as "a clarification of life," yet he shied away from the word *revelation* itself, using it in only two poems—prominently, in the titles. The idea of clarifying, of revealing, however, is all-pervasive in Frost, surfacing in multiple images: stars (especially Sirius), moon, planets, fireflies, a burning bush, broad sunlight, a cathode ray, luminescent crystal rocks, spring pools, a pasture spring, clearing storms, a forest clearing. Still, a definition of *revelation* eludes us; when we ask what Frost meant by it, we inevitably find ourselves trying to place him in some philosophical pigeonhole, while aware that he cannot finally be forced into any. The problem of philosophy arises because *revelation* (beyond its simplest colloquial usage) involves ways-of-knowing—the province of epistemology. Was Frost a monist, a dualist, part Platonist, empiricist? In other words, what were the origins of truth, the paths of knowledge by which he thought revelation came? What were the limits of such knowledge?

"All Revelation," in the seventh volume of poetry, is riddled with ambiguity; the early "Revelation" (though it gains significance from the lustre of the later poem) seems a light-hearted trifle. However diverse in tone, the poems contain some common elements: an abiding need for communication, the persistent obstacles in its way. The metaphor in the earlier piece is a "hide-and-seek" game; the later begins with the image of a difficult, head-first birth, and pursues the figure as the intellect struggles to understand the physical world.

Both poems deal with an interaction of minds. We noted in Chapter II that Frost addresses himself to this theme also in his Introduction to *King Jasper*, where he speaks of "establishing correspondence" in infancy, first by eye-contact, then by vocal contact, and finally by minds reaching for each other.

The terms *revelation* and *correspondence*, in the sense of *communication*, are interrelated in Frost; in particular, he associated revelation with unexpected, free play of metaphor. He called a poem "a revelation, or a series of revelations, as much for the poet as for the reader" ("The Figure a Poem Makes"):

It must be more felt than seen ahead like prophecy. . . . For it to

be that there must have been the greatest freedom of the material
to move about in it and to establish relations in it regardless of time
and space, previous relation, and everything but affinity.

The idea of freshness in metaphor may remind us of Henri
Bergson in his concept of "God" as the essence of freely creating
energy, and of man as the vehicle through whom this inventive
force gains expression. Indeed there is a very Bergsonian passage
in a long narrative poem where Frost extols as God-like play the
metaphoric freedom that artists enjoy:

> For God himself the height of feeling free
> Must have been his success in simile
> When at sight of you he thought of me.

"How Hard It Is to Keep from Being King When It's in You and in
the Situation," where these lines occur, calls the instant of making
metaphor the "perfect moment of unbafflement"—"Freedom to
flash off into wild connections."

The attribution here of figurative play to God is witty—an apparent throw-away idea, as it may seem also in "Revelation." The
implication, however, in "All Revelation," of an entire universe
laced together symbolically cannot be dismissed. It is not tossed
off as an aside; it is the core and substance of the poem—even
though its meaning is complex. Intellectual intensity and rigor of
design demand uncompromised scrutiny. We are left, on one
hand, with whimsical hints that God plays with metaphor; on the
other, with a weighty paradox—that the world is somehow a constant, if enigmatic, symbol. Was Frost's penchant for analogy
merely an *artistic* choice, or did it spring from deep-rooted conviction? In "A Missive Missile" he juggles the question:

> How anyone can fail to see
> Where perfectly in form and tint
> The metaphor, the symbol lies!
> Why will I not analogize?
> (I do too much in some men's eyes.)

We can, in part, understand Frost's use of symbols in the context of the religious heritage—both immediate and remote—from which he came. What were the forces that shaped his thinking? In his childhood there was the Swedenborgian church where his mother was a member. There was also his lifelong admiration for the writings of Ralph Waldo Emerson. And behind Emerson and Swedenborg were the Bible, which Frost knew intimately, and the whole Judeo-Christian tradition.

In that tradition, we find two basic kinds of revelation: scriptural and natural. Scriptural revelation focuses on Old Testament archetypes, or "antitypes," which prefigure New Testament events; for example, the Puritan "errand into the wilderness" (to echo Perry Miller) was a "type" of exodus from Egypt to the promised land. In "natural typology," by contrast, objects in *nature* are seen as emblems, signs of divine meanings.

We find natural revelation in the Bible itself—in the psalmist who sings, "The Heavens declare the glory of God; and the firmament showeth his handiwork." It is in this natural tradition that we may understand Frost. Though well grounded in scripture, he turned, like Emerson, to nature for vital inspiration. "In the woods," Emerson said, "we return to reason and faith." Frost, too, went alone into woods—in the poems he placed first and last in his total works. He wanted living experience for "truths not yet brought to book"; and his "last look" ("One More Brevity") was "taken outside a house and book."

Frost acknowledged Emerson as the thinker most influential in his development. (Second was Emerson's partial disciple, William James.) The American Puritans—nonconformists, Lawrance Thompson reminds us—loomed, in turn, over Emerson, more than he perhaps would have thought or conceded, and lent their weight, at a remove, to Frost, who boasted of his Puritan descent. Like the iconoclast Emerson, Frost was staunchly individual—as Thompson says, "a nonconforming Puritan nonconformist."

Both men, emerging from the Puritanism of New England, seem to reject institutionalized religion—especially the strict Calvinist insistence that scriptural reading is the only valid source of divine revelation. Yet even among the Puritan writers themselves there are distinct leanings toward the counter-tradition of finding God in the Book of Nature. Two in particular show this tendency:

the metaphysical poet Edward Taylor and the theologian Jonathan Edwards. Taylor was little known, less influential in his day. He writes:

> The glory of the world slickt up in types
> In all Choise things chosen to typify,
> His glory upon whom the worke doth light,
> To thine's a Shaddow, or a butterfly.
> How glorious then, my Lord, art thou to mee
> Seing to cleanse me, 's worke alone for thee.

And Edwards, in *Images or Shadows of Divine Things*, perceives natural objects as endowed with allegorical significance:

> I felt God . . . at the first appearance of a thunder storm; and used to take the opportunity, at such times, to fix myself in order to view the clouds, and see the lightnings play, and hear the majestic and awful voice of God's thunder, . . .

Explaining "the basic continuance" from Edwards to Emerson, Perry Miller points to "the incessant drive of the Puritan to learn how, and how most ecstatically, he can hold any sort of communion with the environing wilderness." "The real difference" between these thinkers, Miller asserts:

> lies not in the fact that Edwards was a Calvinist while Emerson rejected all systematic theologies, but in the quite other fact that Edwards went to nature, in all passionate love, convinced that man could receive from it impressions which he must then try to interpret, whereas Emerson went to Nature, no less in love with it, convinced that in man there is a spontaneous correlation with the received impressions.[1]

As to the impact Edwards unwittingly had on Puritan thought, another critic comments:

> If Edwards had attempted to hold in balance a reading of scripture through type and antitype, he had also released a psychological force in New England that would soon destroy altogether the reading of scripture as a primary source of spiritual revelation. God was

not dead; but for the transcendentalist the Word was lifeless until it could be demonstrated that some correspondence existed between the truths of scripture and the spritual ideas revealed in the natural universe.[2]

The intellectual line becomes clear—from the Puritan theologian Edwards who endeavored to cling to orthodox Calvinism, to the transcendentalist Emerson who thought he divested himself of doctrinal trappings, and through Emerson, on to Robert Frost, who, from reading Emerson's *Representative Men,* mixed in more than a dash of Swedenborgianism. Of his mystic side, Frost said:

> What's my philosophy? That's hard to say. I was brought up a Swedenborgian. I am not a Swedenborgian now. But there's a good deal of it that's left with me. I am a mystic. I believe in symbols. I believe in change and in changing symbols.[3]

Swedenborg's "Doctrine of Correspondence" (between the visible and invisible world) left its mark on Frost, as did Emerson's analogical mode of thinking (*Nature,* 1836):

> It is easily seen that there is nothing lucky or capricious in these analogies, but that they are constant, and pervade nature. These are not the dreams of a few poets, here and there, but man is an analogist, and studies relations in all objects. He is placed in the centre of beings, and a ray of relation passes from every other being to him. And neither can man be understood without these objects, nor these objects without man. All the facts in natural history taken by themselves, have no value, but are barren, like a single sex. But marry it to human history, and it is full of life. . . . Throw a stone into the stream, and the circles that propagate themselves are the beautiful type of all influence.

Emerson, like Frost, depended upon a collaboration between man and nature as a means of knowing. Emerson's application of "constant" to "analogies" anticipates Frost's essay "The Constant Symbol," even if Frost carries the idea in a rather different direction. Emerson's "ray of relation" surfaces in Frost's ray-of-light imagery: "We were not given eyes or intellect/For all the light at once the source of light . . ." (*A Masque of Mercy*). And Emerson's "marry[ing]" "natural" and "human history" deepens our understanding of "West-Running Brook," about which more will be said later.

For Emerson—at least, in his moments of transcendental clarity—natural *analogies* were *easily seen*. Frost, by contrast, found Nature's Book difficult to decipher. "All Revelation" testifies to that. He did not scan the visible world as Emerson's "dial plate of the invisible." Yet there was a residual tendency in Frost to view natural events as spiritually emblematic. He knew the concept of *types* and he was drawn to God's figuring forth symbolically in the universe. I once heard him—irritated with modern literary jargon—say testily, "I hate that word *symbol*. I'd change it to *typification*." (He added, "I'm a typical idealist—I'm unscrupulous!") He was humorously defending a tradition where symbols, as Emerson asserted, are not "capricious"—not mere figures of speech—but divine signs, revelations.

Like Keeper in the masque, Frost's "light" was "reflected from the . . . bed of world-flowers," as well as from "the printed page." Though he would not vouch for an accurate reading, the Book of Nature was certainly his text. "Time Out," a finely crafted sonnet, takes its metaphor from the theory of natural types. A mountainside becomes Nature's manuscript; and wildflowers going to seed, "fingered" like pages in a book, are "read" as living figures of the ongoing cycle of death and rebirth. Revelations in Frost are obliquely given; perennial truths that survive fitful sectarian "clamor" are contemplated at a "slant":

> It took that pause to make him realize
> The mountain he was climbing had the slant
> As of a book held up before his eyes
> (And was a text albeit done in plant).
> Dwarf cornel, gold-thread, and maianthemum,
> He followingly fingered as he read,
> The flowers fading on the seed to come;
> But the thing was the slope it gave his head:
> The same for reading as it was for thought,
> So different from the hard and level stare

Of enemies defied and battles fought.
It was the obstinately gentle air
That may be clamored at by cause and sect
But it will have its moment to reflect.

The concept of revelation takes Frost across many avenues of
knowledge. It depends upon acute sensory perception; it involves
also an emblematic turn of mind. For Frost is Emerson's heir. His
inheritance is not just a rag-tail collection of figurative phrases—
what Joseph Warren Beach calls "the aura of New England transcendentalism without a trace of its philosophy." (In the same
breath Beach labels Frost "a refined modern agnostic.") Emerson's legacy to Frost was his essential vision, though Frost gave it
down-to-earthiness.

Frost's difference from Emerson was more quantitative than
qualitative; it was a matter of emphasis, of style, of poetic attitude. His head was less in the clouds, though his gaze pierced the
night for stars. Frost was a self-proclaimed "symbolist" (in the
philosophical, not literary, sense). He wrote Louis Untermeyer in
1917:

I wish for a joke I could do myself, shifting the trees entirely from
the Yankee realist to the Scotch symbolist.

Emerson deplored "a foolish consistency . . . [as] the hobgoblin
of little minds." Frost, too, it seems, wanted things both ways.

Emerson's physical universe may seem at times a mirage—
mere "shows" and "shadows" of a higher spiritual presence. Frost,
by contrast, stands fast on *terra firma*. But his empirically tested
bedrock is unfailingly spiritual; it is composed (although the two
are often indistinguishable) of earthy granite and fallen stars ("A
Star in a Stone-Boat").

In our mind's ear, when we have long forgotten Emerson's pre-
cise language, we still hear tones lofty and sonorous. Frost, too,
could wax oracular, but he spoke in many other voices as well. He
used dramatic counter-tones to challenge the solemnity of certitude. Playfulness to him was both manner and means: metaphoric
play, his way of clarifying life; playfulness of wit, his actor's dis-

guise. Difficulties of poetic interpretation arise when these dual purposes seem *cross*-purposes—to the impatient, even a double-cross.

Lyric lightness may let us dismiss "Revelation" as the expression of a self-indulgent, passing mood of youth. But the deliberately named "All Revelation," which prompted us to give the earlier poem a second look, shows the intellectual depths Frost plumbed in his continuing preoccupation with the problem of "correspondence." Here the question of divine revelation, never raised overtly, informs image and structure. The poem makes no claim for clarification as either absolute or infallible, but it affirms a potential "ray" of light:

> A head thrusts in as for the view,
> But where it is it thrusts in from
> Or what it is it thrusts into
> By that Cyb'laean avenue,
> And what can of its coming come,
>
> And whither it will be withdrawn,
> And what take hence or leave behind,
> These things the mind has pondered on
> A moment and still asking gone.
> Strange apparition of the mind!
>
> But the impervious geode
> Was entered, and its inner crust
> Of crystals with a ray cathode
> At every point and facet glowed
> In answer to the mental thrust.
>
> Eyes seeking the response of eyes
> Bring out the stars, bring out the flowers,
> Thus concentrating earth and skies
> So none need be afraid of size.
> All revelation has been ours.

"All Revelation" is a rhetorical enactment of the difficulty of correspondence between man and the universe—and, also, between poet and reader, for both of whom, we know, Frost wanted *every* poem to be a "revelation." In the first nine lines (a single sentence) the reader is buffeted from question to question— "where," "what," "whither"—and must run a syntactic obstacle course that dizzies at every turn, leaving much to "ponder on." The triple "thrust"—of birth, (prior) sexual intercourse, and inquiring mind—insistently states the ceaseless probing of man's intellect into the material world.

At the end of the second stanza the journey through the verbal thicket leads to a perfect ambiguity. As Reuben Brower notes, the tenth line can be interpreted two ways: that mental activity itself is ephemeral, a "fleeting occurrence"; that what the mind "thrusts into"—so-called physical reality—is an unsubstantial, "ghost-like mode of being." We are confounded by "apparitions" as nebulous as Emerson's "shows" and "shadows." The mystery that is mind, coming through the dark passageway of Cybele, earth-mother-goddess, or through the birth canal, confronts the mystery that is matter, "the impervious geode." (The poem was originally titled "Geode," a word from Greek, meaning *earthlike*. Contrary to the title-change for "Dust of Snow," here the movement was toward, rather than away from, religious suggestiveness.)

In the first stanza, a *but* starts a series of grammatical barriers. The same word at the beginning of the third stanza, by contrast, turns the poem from a course of uncertainty to one of assurance, as if one were "butted" again in a new direction. Here at last, since the poem begins *in medias res*, we encounter the central image, a commonplace nodule of stone that "glowed" from within. Externally ordinary, the stone has an internal cavity lined with crystals. When activated by a cathode ray piercing the seemingly impenetrable surface, the crystals become luminescent with all the spectrum colors.

The "geode" is a synecdochic miniature of the earth—a figure "concentrating" the globe itself. And the poem is a rhetorical demonstration of revelation as mental interaction. The reader must penetrate the obstinate language of the first two stanzas to arrive at an image of wonder and beauty. Persistent thrust of intellect—by the reader, on one level; on another, by mankind in an obdurate universe—is "answer[ed]" by an unforeseen radiance.

The metaphorical argument suggests three properties of "revelation." First, it proceeds upon what Frost called "believing ahead of your evidence." Faith that the undertaking will prove worthwhile must precede man's indefatigable effort to understand his world. Revelation is "more felt than seen ahead"; and even when hidden facets of truth come into view, ultimate understanding is not possible in this life. Until the geode is cracked open, the existence of its inner crystals can be known only by inference. Frost emphasized the distinction between "confidence"—based on empirical knowledge—and "faith." "All great people did everything before they knew enough."[4] "What was the evidence," he asked, "I could write a poem?"[5] Faith is an inherent bond between poetry and religion ("Education by Poetry"):

> The person who gets close enough to poetry, he is going to know more about the word *belief* than anybody else knows, even in religion nowadays. There are two or three places where we know belief outside of religion.

He went on to name these "places" as "the self-belief, the love-belief, and the art-belief." Science, too, we may infer from "All Revelation," depends upon "believing things *in*"—an attitude which is distinct from, and prior to, *believing in things.* (Frost very likely saw this attitude in William James' *The Will to Believe.*)

Second, in the metaphor of the poem, revelation is arrived at by indirection, by interposition of a cathode ray. Man must learn to use a physical law that already exists in order to bring to light a crystalline structure—a design that awaits his discovery.

Finally, illumination is multi-faceted. It is not a single white light—not the searing "Truth . . . [that] burns your eyes out" of *A Masque of Mercy.* The geode emits an interplay of colored lights the beauty of which is inseparable from their complexity. Everywhere in Frost clarification is partial. But "we know well enough to go ahead with./I mean we seem to know enough to act on" (Job in *A Masque of Reason*).

Stylistically, the ending of "All Revelation" is very unlike its beginning. We are struck by evenly paced rhythms, by freedom from contorted syntax. On closer scrutiny, however, we see that there are pieces missing from this puzzle-game. The last stanza confuses us with disjunctive logic and grammatical ambiguity. We notice that one pair of "eyes" lacks any antecedent (*which* one we cannot tell). One pair presumably belongs to the "view[ing]" head. To what does the other pair refer? If there is collaboration between eye-pairs, lighting up a portion of the universe, whose eyes answer man's? Regardless of antecedence, since the eye-pairs are syntactically interchangeable, we can guess that "seeking" and "response" are not only mutually dependent, but simultaneous.   ·

One significant problem remains: the closing assertion, "All revelation has been ours." Despite its ring of certitude, the line is ambiguous. Some critics read it solipsistically—that "all" man perceives as objective truth is his own anthropomorphic projection. They may have in mind the "godlike" self-image reflected from the well surface in "For Once, Then, Something." But the metaphoric argument in "All Revelation" negates this interpretation. It portrays revelation as undeniably a two-way process. The underlying order of the crystals preceded its discovery by man. Still, the "All" is curious. If we discount reading it as "The only thing we can know about the world is a meaning that we impose upon it," then we are left with "All" in the sense of *totality, completeness*. How can we handle so large a claim? The key to this final puzzle lies in the image of "concentrating earth and skies." "Flowers" and "stars"—through the process of "eye" correspondence—become synecdochic, like the geode itself. Interrelationships proliferate: stars with flowers, man's eyes with "eyes" that light up nighttime skies, human insight with divine vision. (Elsewhere, in "A Question," we have: "A voice said, Look me in the stars . . . ")

In 1925 Frost noted in Elizabeth Sergeant's copy of his *Selected Poems*: "Consumed with stars when I was fifteen, with flowers when I was twenty. Matter of history." And more succinctly, "If it isn't flowers its stars," opposite "Bond and Free." That early poem articulates the dual pull of "earth" and "heaven" and the analogous tension between heart and mind, between love that holds man "thrall" and the flight of thought toward "interstellar

gloom." This dynamic conflict persists throughout Frost's poetry:
the swinger of birches at length decides that "Earth's the right
place for love," while in "The Star-Splitter" the "under-ticket-
agent" sacrifices domestic ties—"burn[s] his house down for the
fire insurance" so as to buy a telescope and "satisfy a life-long curi-
osity/About our place among the infinities." Despite this recurring duality, we find various attempts at fusion. "Bond and Free,"
which treats "Love" and "Thought" as abstractions, ends by asserting a harmony between the two. The more artistically mature
"All Revelation" combines them organically and concretely. The
"head thrust[ing] in as for the view" is the physical thrust of the
infant's head, the thrust of love in sexual union that precedes the
birth, and the "mental thrust" for knowledge, as it is identified
later in the poem. Thus the *way of knowing* in "All Revelation," its
implicit epistemology, involves an interaction of mind and heart.
Knowing is a function of loving, and the universe can be known,
multum in parvo. Between them, "flowers" and "stars," akin to
William Blake's "grain of sand" and "wild flower," contain in
minuscule all that need be understood of earth and sky above.
Synecdochically, revelation is whole, entire.

In 1931 Frost tagged himself "a Synecdochist":

> I started calling myself a Synecdochist when others called them-
> selves Imagists or Vorticists. Always, always a larger significance.
> A little thing touches a larger thing.[6]

On another occasion he explained:

> I believe in what the Greeks called synecdoche: the philosophy of
> the part for the whole; skirting the hem of the goddess. All that an
> artist needs is samples.[7]

The notion of artistic "samples" reminds us of lines in "New
Hampshire"—an *ars poetica* piece about synecdoche:

> Just specimens is all New Hampshire has,
> One each of everything as in a show-case
> Which naturally she doesn't care to sell.

But Frost *did* care to sell, or rather to *give*; he wanted his poems accepted "for keeps." (See his *In the Clearing* dedication.) He offers us *sample* revelations: the water in a narrow well mirrors "the summer heaven" ("For Once, Then, Something"); ephemeral "Spring Pools" "reflect/ The total sky almost without defect"; fallen meteorites "compass" extraterrestrial worlds ("A Star in a Stone-Boat").

For some time, critics have pointed out the *terrifying* aspect of Frost's vision, a kind of existential void that gapes before us in some of the poems, notably "Desert Places" with its "empty spaces/Between stars—on stars where no human race is." He was all too conscious of the impact of twentieth-century science on the human psyche, of the disconcerting physics of Einstein eroding the more stable Newtonian universe; and he diagnosed our Space Age illness in "The Lesson for Today": "Space ails us moderns: we are sick with space." He found that we suffer, as "Build Soil" phrases it, from "cosmical dilation":

> We're so much out that the odds are against
> Our ever getting inside in again.
> But inside in is where we've got to get.

Yet his poetry does offer an alternative to the unspecified terror, the "great misgiving" that science has left us with. "All Revelation" presents a way of coping with metaphysical disorientation; synecdoche, metaphoric *concentration*, is an antidote to spatial vastness, "So none need be afraid of size."

VIII

An Annunciation

"That wave's been standing off this jut of shore
Ever since rivers, I was going to say,
Were made in heaven. It wasn't waved to us."

"It wasn't, yet it was. If not to you
It was to me—in an annunciation."

—"WEST-RUNNING BROOK"

"WEST-RUNNING BROOK"

How might Frost hint at emblematic meanings without asserting their reliability? His reluctance to interpret natural symbols called for poetic strategies. Frequently within a single person he used tones of voice which answered back and forth. Or he created a dialogue between *two* people, a more explicit way to make a double statement. Each speaker could maintain a point of view separate and distinct, and both sides of a controversy could be preserved with complete integrity—neither necessarily winning nor losing.

Cast as a dialogue between husband and wife, "West-Running Brook" demonstrates progression of argument by statement and counter-statement. While their modes of looking at things are initially opposite, they arrive ultimately at a position which goes beyond reconciliation. They come by different routes to a place where contradiction itself is a source of enrichment.

The object of their lovers' quarrel is an unusual phenomenon—a brook that stubbornly flows *away* from the sea. The wife opens the issue:

> "What does it think it's doing running west
> When all the other country brooks flow east
> To reach the ocean? It must be the brook
> Can trust itself to go by contraries
> The way I can with you—and you with me—"

More specifically, the discussion turns upon a spot where the brook is interrupted in its course:

> (The black stream, catching on a sunken rock,
> Flung backward on itself in one white wave,
> And the white water rode the black forever,
> Not gaining but not losing, . . .)

At the outset, a correlation is established between cross-currents in nature and cross-natures in people. The behavior of the brook suggests a disagreement that—because it includes a mutual "trust"—is complementary rather than antagonistic. The wife, more prone than her husband to fanciful indulgence, proposes ritualizing the relationship:

> "As you and I are married to each other,
> We'll both be married to the brook. We'll build
> Our bridge across it, and the bridge shall be
> Our arm thrown over it asleep beside it."

Her wish may seem sheer fantasy, but behind it lies a solid principle, one which Emerson puts forth in his 1836 *Nature* essay (see
pages 77-78). He explains that "natural history . . . [is] barren,
like a single sex" unless we "marry it to human history"; then "it is
full of life."

The wife pursues her thought, further humanizing the brook:

> "Look, look, it's waving to us with a wave
> To let us know it hears me."

And, gently rebuked by her husband's naturalistic denial, she still
insists—now invoking religious terminology—that the brook
waved "in an annunciation." The husband counters with a mild
disparagement about "lady-land" and threatens to drop the subject: "It is your brook! I have no more to say." But for all his level-
headedness, already we suspect his own penchant for myth-
making: "Ever since rivers, I was going to say,/ Were made in
heaven."

Less sentimental than his wife, the man nevertheless presses
physical fact for moral significance. His tendency to symbolize is
more intellectually abstract, while hers is homespun and intuitive.
Pushed to break his silence, he brims with analogies. He reads the
counter-currents in the brook as emblematic of waste and
resistance-to-waste in the universal scheme. We saw a similar anti-
thesis in "The Master Speed," where love defies "the rush of everything to waste" (see page 15). He goes on, musing on the
downward drift of things, and on the impulse backward toward
"beginnings":

> "Speaking of contraries, see how the brook
> In that white wave runs counter to itself.
> It is from that in water we were from
> Long, long before we were from any creature.

Here we, in our impatience of the steps,
Get back to the beginning of beginnings,
The stream of everything that runs away.
Some say existence like a Pirouot
And Pirouette, forever in one place,
Stands still and dances, but it runs away,
It seriously, sadly, runs away
To fill the abyss' void with emptiness."

The man's long, eloquent speech spans centuries of thought to draw upon the Bible and biology—the origin of life in water; upon Heraclitus and Bergson—existence as perpetual flux; upon the materialism of Lucretius—the impending dissolution of nature. "Dances" is probably a reference to Frost's contemporary, Havelock Ellis. (In a 1926 Bryn Mawr talk, "Metaphors," Frost—according to a college reporter—found Ellis' "dance" metaphor "unsatisfactory.")

The husband speaks in sad Lucretian tones of the disintegration of matter; he compares the stream to "existence" flowing toward oblivion:

"It flows beside us in this water brook,
But it flows over us. It flows between us
To separate us for a panic moment.
It flows between us, over us, and *with* us.
And it is time, strength, tone, light, life, and love—
And even substance lapsing unsubstantial;"

Then suddenly he rallies; he checks the deathward sweep:

"The universal cataract of death
That spends to nothingness—and unresisted,
Save by some strange resistance in itself,
Not just a swerving, but a throwing back,
As if regret were in it and were sacred."

At a public reading in 1949, Lawrance Thompson relates, Frost paused after "Not just a swerving" and said to the audience, "as in Lucretius." Here the poem turns from the influence of that ancient Roman to the dominance of a more recent source, Henri Bergson.

Both the wave image and the idea of a vital counterforce to death are found in *Creative Evolution*:

> Life as a whole, from the initial impulsion that thrust it into the world, will appear as a wave which rises, and which is opposed by the descending movement of matter.

To Bergson, life is a composite of "physical" and "psychical existence," each tending in a direction opposite to the other. "Physics," he posits, "is simply psychics inverted." Physics "pushes matter in the direction of spatiality." Of metaphysics he asks, "Should not its own task be, on the contrary, to remount the incline that physics descends, to bring back matter to its origins . . . ?" Speculating as to "the possibility, the necessity even of a process the inverse of materiality," he conceives of psychic energy as a dynamic resistant to physical decline, or decay:

> If it were pure consciousness, *a fortiori* if it were supra-consciousness, it would be pure creative activity. In fact, it is riveted to an organism that subjects it to the general laws of inert matter. But everything happens as if it were doing its utmost to set itself free from these laws. It has not the power to reverse the direction of physical changes, . . . It does, however, behave absolutely as a force would behave which, left to itself, would work in the inverse direction. Incapable of *stopping* the course of material changes downwards, it succeeds in *retarding* it.

Bergson's concept of contrary cosmic forces is evident in "West-Running Brook"—in the husband's concern with reversing what Bergson calls "the descending movement of matter." Like Bergson, he finds resistant creative energy operative throughout nature and epitomized in human consciousness. The downward flowing stream

> "has this throwing backward on itself
> So that the fall of most of it is always
> Raising a little, sending up a little.
> Our life runs down in sending up the clock.
> The brook runs down in sending up our life.

The sun runs down in sending up the brook.
And there is something sending up the sun.
It is this backward motion toward the source,
Against the stream, that most we see ourselves in,
The tribute of the current to the source.
It is from this in nature we are from.
It is most us."

The "something sending up the sun" may remind us, in its im-
personality, of Bergson's vital principle—a "centre from which
worlds shoot out like rockets in a fire-works display." Frost's cau-
tious "that in water we were from" (primordial slime? or the spirit
of God that moved upon the face of the deep?)—and his subsequent "this in nature we are from"—likewise suggest philosophical detachment. Yet there is in "West-Running Brook" a quietly
reverential tone that is absent from *Creative Evolution*. Bergson
calls "the whole of humanity, in space and in time, . . . "

one immense army galloping beside and before and behind each
of us in an overwhelming charge able to beat down every resistance and clear the most formidable obstacles, perhaps even death.

The militant clamor and implied human pride with which Bergson storms the gates of immortality are very different from the
understated devotion binding "current" back to "source" in
Frost's poem. (The word *religion* means *a binding back*.) There
the "wave" of resistance is not a collective seige, but an individual
"tribute"—"As if regret were in it and were sacred."[1]

The poem ends in harmony, with a touch of irony. In a deferen-
tial summary of her husband's philosophical excursion, the
woman concedes, "Today will be the day/You said so." He replies, also conciliatory, "No, today will be the day/ You said the
brook was called West-running Brook." In effect he admits she
had the quicker insight, suggesting the name at the start. The closing line, the wife's, resolves the dramatic tension: "Today will be
the day of what we both said." The integrity of what each has
contributed is to be preserved, commemorated.

The wife's final comment is not mere verbal politeness, for
their underlying agreement is substantial. Her romantic notion of

marriage to the brook is corroborated in her husband's vision of
an indissoluble wedding of mankind to a current of life that
"flows between us, over us, and *with* us." But he has spent his
mental powers to establish the same point she made with a simple
metaphor. By discursive logic he circles back to the place where
she started, when she fancied the brook "waving" to them. The
woman has interpreted the natural sign-language instinctively;
the man's elaborate speculation has, finally, put him in a position
compatible with her apparent foolishness.

In this rounding out, again we discover a parallel to Bergson,
who says of intellection and intuition:

> The truth is, the two procedures are of opposite direction . . . The
> philosopher is obliged to abandon intuition, once he has received
> from it the impetus, and to rely on himself to carry on the move-
> ment by pushing the concepts one after another. But he soon feels
> he has lost foothold; he must come into touch with intuition again;
> he must undo most of what he has done.

"West-Running Brook" clothes Bergsonian abstractions in flesh.
The human pair are indispensable to each other in a grand design
that "Can trust itself to go by contraries." For Frost, mind may
ever probe and analyze, yet the kinship with nature that the heart
feels remains inviolable.

In considering the "grace note" poems we noticed that a sense
of rapport with nature is most intense when it is not cerebral. One
critic has called Frost "anti-intellectual in an intellectual sense,"
giving equal weight to the poet's fondness for rational inquiry and
his reliance upon emotional or psychological "evidence" that defies both empirical test and logical analysis. In the companion
pieces "Two Look at Two" and "The Most of It" these dual tendencies are *not* held in equilibrium; the sensory impact of an event
takes precedence over its full intellectual comprehension. Both
might be termed "visitation" poems, since they deal with animal
visitors and involve a kind of revelation. "One More Brevity,"
with its overnight Dalmatian "guest," could be placed in the same
category. Like the "annunciation" in "West-Running Brook," such
visitations imply an emblematic reading of nature.

"Two Look at Two," in the "Grace Notes" section of *New Hampshire*, centers around yet another "unlooked-for favor." The difference between this, a narrative, and other "grace notes" (essentially lyrics) is ostensibly in genre. However, there is also here an intrinsic difference in the intensity of the experience—the extent of active correspondence between man and animal. A "tumbled wall" roughly marks off their separate zones; it defines physical, but not visual limits. Lines of sight meet, like the response of eyes to eyes in "All Revelation." Over the man-made barrier, two lovers, probably man and wife, confront a pair of deer.

The human pair, with darkness coming on, are about to turn back from further climbing up a mountainside:

> "This is all," they sighed,
> "Good-night to woods." But not so; there was more.
> A doe from round a spruce stood looking at them
> Across the wall, as near the wall as they.
> She saw them in their field, they her in hers.

"Looking" and "seeing," as elsewhere in Frost's poetry, figure prominently.

> The difficulty of seeing what stood still,
> Like some up-ended boulder split in two,
> Was in her clouded eyes: they saw no fear there.

The doe, content "not [to] trouble her mind . . . too long," vanishes into the woods. The unexpected event, the exchange of glances, seems ended.

> "*This*, then, is all. What more is there to ask?"
> But no, not yet. A snort to bid them wait.
> A buck from round the spruce stood looking at them
> Across the wall as near the wall as they.
> This was an antlered buck of lusty nostril,
> Not the same doe come back into her place.

The reiterative "This is all" and "*This*, then, is all" (they "ask" no more; favors are bestowed) call to mind the puzzling assertion at

the end of "All Revelation." And, especially, the ambiguous conclusion of "The Most of It": "and that was all." Frost's uses of *all*
range in implication from minimal (the *only* thing) to maximal
(*everything*), altering the entire meaning of the poems where they
occur.

Having "viewed them quizzically with jerks of head," the buck
turns from the human pair; "he too passed unscared along the
wall."

> Two had seen two, whichever side you spoke from.
> "This *must* be all." It was all. Still they stood,
> A great wave from it going over them,
> As if the earth in one unlooked-for favor
> Had made them certain earth returned their love.

The repeated "Across the wall, as near the wall as they" reinforces the discontinuity between man and nature. But the mutual
"looking" affirms a degree of communication. Like the doe, the
man and wife do not "trouble . . . mind" with questions. Instead, they are inundated in a tide of "love"—overwhelmed by a
sense of communion with "the earth," *as if* the bond were true. But
the emotional validity of the experience may involve a spiritual
validity. Human love—which is presented as *real* in the poem—
may be a catalyst to an equally real spiritual union with nature. To
read these lines naturalistically—the human pair "felt good"—is to
misread the poem. As we learn in "A Prayer in Spring," human
love in Frost is a synecdochic expression of divine love.[2]

In "The Most of It" there is no rapturous return of love. However, the poem dramatizes an encounter with the natural world
that is powerful in psychological impact. The situation described
is totally unlike that in the companion narrative, where the human
lovers—secure in each other's company—see and feel in unison.
Their mood is receptive to love. By contrast, the solitary figure in
"The Most of It" is "alone" *and* lonely. Impatient with life, he cries
out for a sign of recognition:

> He thought he kept the universe alone;
> For all the voice in answer he could wake
> Was but the mocking echo of his own
> From some tree-hidden cliff across the lake.

Some morning from the boulder-broken beach
He would cry out on life, that what it wants
Is not its own love back in copy speech,
But counter-love, original response.
And nothing ever came of what he cried
Unless it was the embodiment that crashed
In the cliff's talus on the other side,
And then in the far distant water splashed,
But after a time allowed for it to swim,
Instead of proving human when it neared
And someone else additional to him,
As a great buck it powerfully appeared,
Pushing the crumpled water up ahead,
And landed pouring like a waterfall,
And stumbled through the rocks with horny tread,
And forced the underbrush—and that was all.

The poem breaks into two parts: the propounding and the enigmatic solution of a problem. The first, two quatrains, presents the double irony of the man's isolation. His solitude, on the one hand, has inspired unwarranted egoism; he imagines himself as stage-manager on the cosmic scene. On the other hand, it has ensnared him in a solipsistic trap; he hears from the wings only the "mocking echo" of his own speech. The phrase "original response" seems a contradiction, but it conveys his double, if paradoxical, need. He wants an answer; he craves also an aboriginal utterance—one that speaks from the source of nature.

The second part begins with a seemingly flat denial of his demand ("And nothing ever came of what he cried . . . "). But the denial is immediately diverted, if not reversed, by the turn-signal "Unless," which—with the lines following—gives the unspecified "It" of the title a tentative meaning. "It" is now vaguely identified as an "embodiment," as if whatever "it" is were a kind of incarnation: "*As* a great buck it powerfully appeared." (Was Frost thinking of Yeats's "The Second Coming"—of the "revelation" there in the "shape" of an amoral "rough beast . . . / Slouch[ing] towards Bethlehem"?).

The contrast in attitude between this creature and the buck in "Two Look at Two" is enormous. In that "visitation" the male deer, while "antlered" and "of lusty nostril," views the lovers "quizzically with jerks of head." If "unscared," he is surely tame, mildly curious. In "The Most of It" the animal projects sheer bestial strength—crashing, splashing, pushing, stumbling, "pouring like a waterfall," and "forc[ing] the underbrush." The world of nature remains alien; the reponse, if it *is* a response, is impersonal, inarticulate, instinctive, amoral.

Yet the force is not totally unknowable; the buck *embodies* relentless energy and, as a type of "revelation," manifests creative and destructive powers at loose in the universe—dynamics operating indifferent to the human need for intelligibility and love. Confronting an entity beyond his understanding or control, the man's initial egoism is shattered.

The equivocal ending ("and that was all") can mean, quite dispassionately: the incident was over; there was nothing further. Or it can voice disappointment: this brute response is less than was expected, hoped for. Or, more positively, more philosophically encompassing: this *appearance*, this incarnation, concentrates in its formidable frame (like Blake's "Tyger") *all* cosmic vitality.

"The Most of It" reinforces the all-but-discontinuous character of Frost's universe—a universe saved from total disconnection by brief moments of empathy between man and nature. One poem, however, "I Will Sing You One-O," dispels this discontinuity more than briefly. It offers a sustained vision of unity. Entranced, we quit for a time the unfixed cosmos of Henri Bergson; we leave the pluralistic configuration of William James, premised upon what he termed "contiguity, or concatenation," rather than "monistic . . . universal co-implication, or integration of all things . . . ". We return to the balanced celestial machine of seventeenth-century astronomy—to the giant clockwork where "a single weight," as Kepler said, "drives all the gears."

"I Will Sing You One-O" takes the clockwork image as its unifying metaphor. The striking of two public clocks in a snowbound town evokes the figure of the astronomic timepiece. Lying sleepless in his bedroom, the man in the poem listens to the hushed night-time sounds of snow and wind outside his window:

> It was long I lay
> Awake that night
> Wishing the tower

Would name the hour
And tell me whether
To call it day
(Though not yet light)
And give up sleep.
The snow fell deep
With the hiss of spray;
Two winds would meet,
One down one street,
One down another,
And fight in a smother
Of dust and feather.
I could not say,
But feared the cold
Had checked the pace
Of the tower clock
By tying together
Its hands of gold
Before its face.

At last, "tower" and "steeple" clocks announce, in succession, the first hour of the coming dawn:

Then came one knock!
A note unruffled
Of earthly weather,
Though strange and muffled
The tower said, "One!"
And then a steeple.
They spoke to themselves
And such few people
As winds might rouse
From sleeping warm
(But not unhouse).
They left the storm
That struck *en masse*
My window glass
Like a beaded fur.

The striking of the clocks carries him in thought out across interplanetary and interstellar space:

In that grave One
They spoke of the sun
And moon and stars,
Saturn and Mars
And Jupiter.
Still more unfettered,
They left the named
And spoke of the lettered,
The sigmas and taus
Of constellations.

The pealing town clocks become celestial surrogates:

They filled their throats
With the furthest bodies
To which man sends his
Speculation,
Beyond which God is;
The cosmic motes
Of yawning lenses.
Their solemn peals
Were not their own:
They spoke for the clock
With whose vast wheels
Theirs interlock.

This perfectly synchronized celestial harmony is interrupted at
the end, with a shift of focus back to earth and to sublunary strife,
where "man . . . drag[s] down man/ And nation nation."

"I Will Sing You One-O"—another of the *New Hampshire*
"Grace Notes"—goes well beyond other "favor" poems to cele-
brate man's communion with the farthest galaxies. However, on
close scrutiny we discover an insistent, if underplayed, counterpoint to the vision of oneness. Technically, the poem asserts two-
ness. It embodies a basic split in Frost's own consciousness: he
called himself "a monist in wish, a dualist in thought." The rhythm
is *dimeter*—a concession to an inherent limitation of regular meter. (A "poem" of single-stress lines would be no more than a
fragmented series of rhymes, or non-rhymes, and no true poem.
There would be no metric grid across which the sound of speech

might cut.) Further, the imagery itself, *two* earthly clocks, recognizes duality. Though each yields a single note, the clocks do not strike in unison. As we know, absolute simultaneity is a physical impossibility, since time is a function of space and two objects cannot occupy the same space at the same time.

"I Will Sing You One-O" is an annunciation poem to the extent that man is "spoken to, favored." But the striking clocks are, after all, man-made and subject to physical laws. They share with all nature in the multiplicity of a universe where time and space are interdependent, but never identical. These two remain coordinate functions on Frost's visionary graph; even in the hush of a snowbound night there is no "still point," as T. S. Eliot put it, where they are absorbed one into the other.

IX

Salvation in Surrender

Here are your waters and your watering place.
Drink and be whole again beyond confusion.

—"DIRECTIVE"

"DIRECTIVE"

The overwhelming question to which all other aspects of Frost's religious speculation lead is probably that of salvation. From the panorama of waste, loss, defeat that the world everywhere presents, can anything be saved? His concern with salvation arises from an intense awareness of material waste. The fading day, the falling year are, partly, metaphors of dashed hope, of exhausted effort, of love that ends in failure—"finalities/Besides the grave" ("The Impulse")—or in death. "Love," he remarked, as he read aloud "Ends" from *In the Clearing*, "can't have a happy ending."

I do not think his interest in salvation was initially theological; it sprang, rather, from his recurring wonder about the meaning of loss and about man's struggles to stave it off—as "November" suggests, by *storing* and *keeping*. While "we make a boast of" these makeshift secular devices for *saving*, they are finally inadequate, and their limitations can lead us to question salvation in ultimate terms. Gradually, for Frost, resistance-to-waste took on religious import—in "West-Running Brook," for example, "As if . . . sacred."

The problem of loss assumes various guises, surfacing as lyric melancholy, as intellectual inquiry, as meditative quest. Frost addresses it plaintively in his final volume:

> Where have those flowers and butterflies all gone
> That science may have staked the future on?

Here, in "Pod of the Milkweed," there is direct confrontation of waste:

> Calling all butterflies of every race
> From source unknown but from no special place
> They ever will return to all their lives,
> Because unlike the bees they have no hives,
> The milkweed brings up to my very door
> The theme of wanton waste in peace and war
> As it has never been to me before.

This encounter has others before it. These butterflies are descendants (by eons in insect time) of the one that inspired Frost's youthful elegy, his first published poem in a national magazine, "My Butterfly," which appeared in *The Independent* in 1894:

> I found that wing broken today!
> For thou art dead, I said,
> And the strange birds say.
> I found it with the withered leaves
> Under the eaves.

Behind "Pod of the Milkweed" lies also "November" with its catalogue of wasted "leaves," "moments," "pleasure," and even "nations." Coming out of a year of world conflict, 1938, "November" builds to a climax in which war is a mournful extension of all that is profligate in nature.

Behind it, too, are other poems, as early as the 1913 book, *A Boy's Will*: "Ghost House" which contains the seed of the later deserted-village poem, "Directive"; "My November Guest," in "praise" of barren trees; "A Late Walk" ("the last remaining aster flower" is picked as a love token); "October," an "amethyst"-tinted retarding of summer; "Reluctance," another fall poem where loss of "love,"mentioned only in the last line and subordinated to the final rhyme, deceptively seems a mere afterthought:

> Ah, when to the heart of man
>   Was it ever less than a treason
> To go with the drift of things,
>   To yield with a grace to reason,
> And bow and accept the end
>   Of a love or a season?

As "Reluctance" so delicately hints, human sorrow is inevitable in the natural scheme; the understated "drift of things" anticipates the more devastating "universal cataract of death" in "West-Running Brook." Yet Frost was fond of dusk ("my time of day," he calls it in "The Wind and the Rain") and autumn; he was attracted equally to the decline and to the birth of things. Especially in his early poetry he found melancholy pleasure "in this air of withering sweetness" ("Waiting"). Already "in the springing of the year" he looked wistfully toward "the uncertain harvest" ("A Prayer in Spring").

Predictably, the "happy sadness" of Frost's youth darkened to a bleaker vision of pain and suffering. But tragedy itself somehow gives shape to life ("The Wind and the Rain"):

> Oh, should a child be left unwarned
> That any song in which he mourned
> Would be as if he prophesied?
> It were unworthy of the tongue
> To let the half of life alone
> And play the good without the ill.
> And yet 'twould seem that what is sung
> In happy sadness by the young
> Fate has no choice but to fulfill.

These lines, published when Frost was seventy-two, may be read as a sober response to Robert Browning's cheerfulness about old age in "Rabbi Ben Ezra." Frost is not pessimistic, though; he is realistic, trusting:

> That far-off day the leaves in flight
> Were letting in the colder light.
> A season-ending wind there blew
> That as it did the forest strew
> I leaned on with a singing trust
> And let it drive me deathward too.

The persistent iambic beat—punctuated by the heavily stressed "Fate has no choice . . . "—reflects steadfastness and the will not only to believe in life, but to *sing* about it. In "Away!"—the lyrical death prophecy from *In the Clearing*—Frost was still singing.

No stranger to loss, Frost was fascinated by the subject. "You wouldn't know," he once said of "November," according to George Nitchie, "that here I was praising waste." In his later years he pinpointed this fascination as "some dim secret of the good of waste" ("Pod of the Milkweed"); where others might have inferred futility in life, he looked for purpose:

> the reason why so much
> Should come to nothing must be fairly faced.

The preoccupation with waste is always there, at times under-
scored with brash humor; he writes Louis Untermeyer in 1931:

> We are in many many troubles for the moment, so many that grief
> loses its dignity and bursts out laughing. I toughen, it seems to me.
> Of course I may be prejudiced in my own favor, but if I keep on I
> think I can't be refused a chance for the heavyweight crown. . . . I
> used to say yes I'm ready to fight, but I don't want my teeth broken.
> Well, I was wrong. What reason had I for not having my teeth
> broken? . . . We were brought up on principles of saving every-
> thing, ourselves included. The war taught us a new gospel. My next
> book is to be called The Right to Waste. The Right? The duty, the
> obligation, to waste everything, time, material, *and* the man.

In a less pugnacious mood, Frost offers a practical formula for
dealing with loss, one that served him well in life and poetry:
"Strongly spent is synonymous with kept" ("The Constant Symbol"). The conviction is latent in many situations. Baptiste, the
French Canadian woodcutter in "The Ax-Helve" "knew how to
make a short job long/ For love of it, and yet not waste time
either." The best way to counter loss is to love a task, whether
splitting wood or writing poems. Frost's "one ambition," he often
said, was "to write a few poems it would be hard to get rid of." He
dedicated *In the Clearing* with a somewhat cryptic inscription
which ends, "for keeps." With "love" joined to "need," a man's
deeds *stay* "done" ("Two Tramps in Mud Time"). He may waste
himself physically in his labor, and "Time" ("The Grindstone")
may have the final decision as to the *completion* of his efforts, but
the ultimate *completeness* of a man's striving is measured by the
sense of fulfillment gained from a life "strongly spent." "I'd rather
do *well*," Frost said at Bread Loaf toward the end of his life, "than
do good." To do something well is to save the best in us from the
onslaught of death. "I could give all to Time," the poem of that
title asserts,

> —except
> What I myself have held. But why declare

The things forbidden that while the Customs slept
I have crossed to Safety with? For I am There,
And what I would not part with I have kept.

"Storing" and "keeping," from "November," and here "Safety"
are all members of a verbal matrix shaping Frost's concept of salvation. Anywhere that man's spiritual essence—what "is most us,"
as "West-Running Brook" puts it—survives the ravages of time,
salvation is at issue. Man's intellect shall have final dominion,
"Sand Dunes" insists; through his "mind" shall man defy the ebb
and flow of mortality:

> Sea waves are green and wet,
> But up from where they die,
> Rise others vaster yet,
> And those are brown and dry.
>
> They are the sea made land
> To come at the fisher town,
> And bury in solid sand
> The men she could not drown.
>
> She may know cove and cape,
> But she does not know mankind
> If by any change of shape,
> She hopes to cut off mind.
>
> Men left her a ship to sink:
> They can leave her a hut as well;
> And be but more free to think
> For the one more cast-off shell.

Throughout Frost's poetry, salvation is not something that man
passively receives. True, it is a gift and cannot be earned. But it is a
reciprocal giving. In the hope (but with no guarantee) of being
saved, man must fully dedicate himself to whatever it is he be-
lieves in. Created "free to think," he must vigorously engage his
intellect. Most important, he must summon all his "courage,"
which—Keeper in *A Masque of Mercy* reminds us—"is of the
heart by derivation." ("Courage" comes from the Latin *cor*, mean-

ing *heart*. "Our sacrifice," to repeat Paul's words, must be "the best we have to offer."

Salvation, like revelation, involves man's taking an active role to make the idea a reality. This imperative is made explicit in "The Gift Outright," which returns to the theme of preserving through labors of love what a man most values. Once again, salvation is connected to wholeness of being, a concept that here is carried into the realm of *re*integration, rebirth. Premised upon "believing things *in*" (in this case, a nation), the poem explores the paradox of repossession of the self through self-surrender. Newly arrived Englishmen in colonial America—and, later, their pioneer descendants—had to relinquish their identity as strangers to this continent. Emotionally and psychologically, they had to make a total commitment to a land that their gift of self, alone, could make their own—could make *real*. And in this act they themselves were redeemed. They found self-realization, "salvation":

> The land was ours before we were the land's.
> She was our land more than a hundred years
> Before we were her people. She was ours
> In Massachusetts, in Virginia,
> But we were England's, still colonials,
> Possessing what we still were unpossessed by,
> Possessed by what we now no more possessed.
> Something we were withholding made us weak
> Until we found out that it was ourselves
> We were withholding from our land of living,
> And forthwith found salvation in surrender.
> Such as we were we gave ourselves outright
> (The deed of gift was many deeds of war)
> To the land vaguely realizing westward,
> But still unstoried, artless, unenhanced,
> Such as she was, such as she would become.

The subject matter is political, not explicitly religious. But the paradox unmistakably relates to the Christian precept of losing one's life in a material sense, to find it in a spiritual sense. The poem is not necessarily advancing a corollary of Christian doctrine, although as John Robert Doyle, Jr., observes, the phrase

"Such as we were" and the idea of finding "salvation in surrender" strike "the note of humility so important to Christianity." Of course, the hope of being born again is central to the New Testament. Not here or elsewhere, however, do I choose to push Frost into the Christian camp, despite its closeness to his thinking, and regardless of his absorption of Christian attitudes—especially as they are channelled through American Puritanism. Nevertheless, the poem is fundamentally religious. "The Founding Fathers," Frost told an interviewer about twenty years after its composition, " . . . believed [the future] *in*."[1] "The Gift Outright" celebrates an act of faith in things unseen.

Chapter VI dealt with finding salvation in a sense of wholeness; "Kitty Hawk" tells us how "We may get control" of experience through metaphor. There we did not treat the problem of loss in relation to salvation. The regained wholeness in "The Gift Outright," on the other hand, takes loss into account. Here, as in "Directive," relinquishment and reintegration go hand in hand. But the way to salvation remains the same throughout Frost's poetry: to find the figure that gives shape to one's life is to discover and to save oneself. For the venturesome settlers in "The Gift Outright" the figure lay ahead, with "the land vaguely realizing westward." For the solitary traveller in "Directive" the shaping metaphor has to be retraced through the past, his own and that of all life back to the beginning.

"Directive" is Frost's quintessential poem on salvation, on the meaning of wholeness. The two masques may be, as he claimed, his "old" and "new testament," but "Directive" is his most penetrating, if most perplexing, religious statement. Many of his prior poems, unwittingly, anticipate it; those that follow must be read in the light of its existence. What "The Gift Outright" ponders— recovery of self through an active acceptance of loss—"Directive" dramatizes. The poem does not offer salvation in strictly Christian terms, but it does not rule out Christian conversion as a viable means of being saved. (Reuben Brower disagrees, since it ignores the concept of sin-repentence-forgiveness.) "Directive" abandons all easy formulas. In fact, its basic difficulty is that it abandons almost *everything* in order to make us "whole again beyond confusion." "Directive" is a sacramental journey into the depths of self, and back through historical and geological ages. It moves beyond "Kitty Hawk," where "wholeness" is attained "by craft or art." "Directive" leaves *crafty* man, prudential man, altogether behind. In the language of "Provide, Provide," it relies "on being simply true." And the utter simplicity that is the goal of this journey confounds us.

The internal quest undertaken in "Directive" originates in Frost's younger imagination, at least as early as "Into My Own" in *A Boy's Will*. The external landscape that merges with internal terrain as the past is recaptured, is also reached by previous poetic markers—for example, the interstellar "empty spaces" of the soul in "Desert Places" and, much earlier, the awesome loneliness that Rob Frost, a boy in San Francisco, felt in the "shattered . . . waves" of an oncoming storm "Once by the Pacific." (A note in *West-Running Brook* dates the poem—or the event recorded—"As of about 1880.") In this, another poem about endings, the breaking waves suggest an impending end of the world:

> There would be more than ocean-water broken
> Before God's last *Put out the Light* was spoken.

Further, "Directive" encompasses the *wreckage* of loss, of things "shattered," like its playhouse "dishes", and "broken," like its "drinking goblet". Quite specifically, it echoes the "broken drinking glass" at the spring in "The Times Table." In metaphoric reach it comprehends the delicate "broken" wing of the butterfly in Frost's early elegy and the violently "broken shaft" in "The Draft Horse." It includes the "broken sleep" of the woman in "The Night Light," "the broken moon" that is an extension of broken sleep in "An Old Man's Winter Night," Silas' "broken" spirit in "The Death of the Hired Man," and, from "The Lesson for Today," all our "broken-off careers":

> The earth itself is liable to the fate
> Of meaninglessly being broken off.

Behind "Directive," and behind Frost's extensive imagery of loss elsewhere, is a pervasive awareness of the vanity of human desire, leading us back to the vision in Ecclesiastes (12:6) of "the golden bowl" that is "broken," "the pitcher . . . broken at the fountain, . . . the wheel broken at the cistern."

The journey in "Directive" is the culmination of many lonely wanderings among landmarks eroded, burned out, dissolved, vanished: the abandoned "cellar hole" of "The Generations of Men," the deserted "black-paper-covered house" in "The Census-Taker," the house consumed by flames and the all-but-forsaken barn in "The Need of Being Versed in Country Things", where phoebes fly through "broken windows." It is a journey, however, on which acceptance of loss becomes a principle of renewal, a means to spiritual reintegration. The symbol of revitalization is the spring water at the end of the quest, where we are led to rediscover our beginnings. "People miss the key to the poem," Frost told his friend Hyde Cox,

> the key lines, if you want to know, are 'Cold as a spring as yet so near its source,/ Too lofty and original to rage.' . . . But the key word in the whole poem is source—whatever source it is.

Denying a restrictive Christian meaning, Frost explained what he meant by "source":

> The poet is not offering any general salvation—nor Christian salvation in particular. In the midst of this now too much for us he tells everyone to go back . . . to whatever source they have. The source might even be a conventional religion . . . but religion is most of all valuable when something original has been contributed to it.[2]

Critics have variously interpreted the "source" in "Directive." Margaret Blum views it Biblically, as representing "the living God" of pre-institutional religion—the "fundamental Truth" back beyond "the two lost cultures" of "possibly" Judaism and "certainly" Christianity. In a pastoral vein, Elizabeth Shepley Sergeant suggests the "spiritual guide" is "a sort of high shepherd," and the life-giving waters are an "arcane spring, perhaps Pierian?" Pursuing classical allusion further, Helen Bacon connects the wa-

ter image to "the spring of the Muses on Mt. Parnassus." Theodore
Morrison relies less upon Biblical or classical resonances, equating
"source" with "poetry in the largest sense." Reuben Brower sees
"Directive" as arriving "at salvation not through embracing a doctrine or through argument . . . but through poetry." He calls the
recovered wholeness " 'a moral equivalent' of salvation."

I take exception to Brower's "moral equivalent," for wholeness
in the poem is not *virtually similar* to religious salvation; it is essentially *the same*. Understanding metaphor—finding the vital figure
that makes one's life meaningful in or out of traditional faith—is
the key to salvation in "Directive." The ritual, parable, and myth
of the Bible deal in *symbolic* truth, like all poetry. Christ (Saint
Mark, 9:41) speaks of the giving of "a cup of water to drink in
[His] name" as a sign that the giver "shall not lose his reward." Any
drink that quenches man's spiritual thirst and makes him *whole*, is,
like the one offered in "Directive," *holy*.

While "Directive" sets up guideposts for us on a communal pil-
grimage back to lost innocence, the healing waters we long to find
must spring from our own inner resources and nourish us individ-
ually. For some, the vision of childlike simplicity toward which
the poem directs us will include Christ's injunction to his disciples
to become as "little children." (The relevance of Saint Mark's gospel is made clear at the end of the poem.) Of the backward
movement to innocence, Frost comments (again to Cox):

> The waters and the watering place are the source. It is there that
> you would have to turn in time of confusion to be made whole
> again: whole again as perhaps you haven't been since leaving
> childhood behind. Aging, you have become involved in the cob-
> webs and considerations of the world.

The term "cobwebs" calls to mind the early "Birches" with its
romantic climber growing "weary of considerations," finding
"life . . . too much like a pathless wood/ Where your face burns
and tickles with the cobwebs/ Broken across it . . . ." But the
distance from "Birches" (1915) to "Directive" (1946) cannot be
measured on the calendar. "Birches" is a playful excursion *"Toward* heaven" and back. "Directive" is a "serial ordeal" across an
arduous landscape.

The invitation to the journey is disconcerting, issued by "a guide . . . / Who only has at heart your getting lost." (Contrast the ingenuous "You come too" of "The Pasture.") At the outset he seems determined to lead us astray:

> Back out of all this now too much for us,
> Back in a time made simple by the loss
> Of detail, burned, dissolved, and broken off
> Like graveyard marble sculpture in the weather,
> There is a house that is no more a house
> Upon a farm that is no more a farm
> And in a town that is no more a town.

Under the guise of simplicity we are offered syntactic complexity (the delayed subject) and confusing imagery. Eradication of detail is a strange mode of clarification. In this "broken off" terrain of a vanished era we are already well on our way to lostness. Our destination is obscure and our only signposts are the barren remains of a weathered past: "The road there . . . / May seem as if it should have been a quarry—"

> Great monolithic knees the former town
> Long since gave up pretense of keeping covered.
> And there's a story in a book about it:
> Besides the wear of iron wagon wheels
> The ledges show lines ruled southeast northwest,
> The chisel work of an enormous Glacier
> That braced his feet against the Arctic Pole.
> You must not mind a certain coolness from him
> Still said to haunt this side of Panther Mountain.

Our perspective is shifting. We read in the "book" of geology a wordless scripture. Juxtaposed to human history ("iron wagon wheels") are the record of a prehistoric ice age and the haunting presence, in the fringes of a polar ice cap, of some legendary deity—like the Biblical Yahweh, reputed to have originated as a mountain god—perhaps matching "coolness" to man's indifference. (On the Biblically named "Hor" in "The Mountain" there is, at or near the summit, an elusive "spring" that also suggests a constant principle surviving change.)

Gradually the landscape comes more alive; human ghosts peer from "cellar holes" and the woods "rustle" with "excitement" of "upstart inexperience"—"Where were they all not twenty years ago?" We feel linked in spirit to those who travelled "ahead" on this homeward trek. The customary notion of the past as *behind* is reversed.

> Make yourself up a cheering song of how
> Someone's road home from work this once was,
> Who may be just ahead of you on foot
> Or creaking with a buggy load of grain.

At last, the "height of the adventure" is reached; it is

> the height
> Of country where two village cultures faded
> Into each other. Both of them are lost.
> And if you're lost enough to find yourself
> By now, pull in your ladder road behind you
> And put a sign up CLOSED to all but me.

Symbolically, the high point of our quest is at the nadir of loss. Accepting a self-imposed isolation, we are then told to "make [ourselves] at home" in this alien land which is to become a native country of spiritual rebirth.

In a "field/ . . . no bigger than a harness gall" we encounter the remnants of two vanished houses—"the children's house of make believe," perhaps the repository of forgotten dreams, and "a belilaced cellar hole,/ Now slowly closing like a dent in dough." This had been "a house in earnest," that someone built, we may suppose, by the sweat of his brow. We are to be nourished by the water of the real house, "A brook . . . / Cold as a spring as yet so near its source,/ Too lofty and original to rage." But we must drink from a mysteriously concealed vessel, shaped by the imagination and "broken" by reality:

> I have kept hidden in the instep arch
> Of an old cedar at the waterside
> A broken drinking goblet like the Grail

Under a spell so the wrong ones can't find it,
So can't get saved, as Saint Mark says they mustn't.
(I stole the goblet from the children's playhouse.)
Here are your waters and your watering place.
Drink and be whole again beyond confusion.

With the recovery of the Grail-like vessel and our drinking of the living spring, the poem ends, and with it our quest. The "goblet" is a multivalent symbol. It evokes, of course, the Medieval knight errant. The reference to the Gospel invites Christian parallels, but we may recall that Frost liked to extend Saint Mark's assertion, paraphrasing it as "You can't be saved unless you understand poetry" (see Chapter VI, n. 1). The goblet may represent for some readers the "hidden" significance of Biblical parable, but, more inclusively, it embodies the ability to play—to experience wholeness through play with metaphor. Although the children's playthings are physically "shattered," their "house of make believe"—conceived in the imagination—is inviolate.

Salvation in "Directive" rests on paradox. The guide's technique of getting the reader "lost" in order to "find" himself can be compared to the Christian idea of going through the gateway of death to reach eternal life. Attaining salvation by suffering was the way of the martyrs, and of Christ on the road to Calvary. To "Weep for what little things could make [the children] glad" is to share in the poignancy of sorrow from which innocence itself is not exempt. Finally, the wholesome waters are to be drunk from a "broken" vessel. Yeats's lines come to mind (they exist in a quite different context):

> For nothing can be sole or whole
> That has not been rent.

The goblet, stolen "from the children's playhouse," is a metaphor of rediscovered innocence. It is also the cup of woe from which we must drink to be saved—an emblem of wholeness regained through endurance of loss; an emblem of the "Heaven" we are given (see page 40) "if we own up broken."[3]

X

The Trial by Existence

And from a cliff-top is proclaimed
  The gathering of the souls for birth,
The trial by existence named,
  The obscuration upon earth.

—"THE TRIAL BY EXISTENCE"

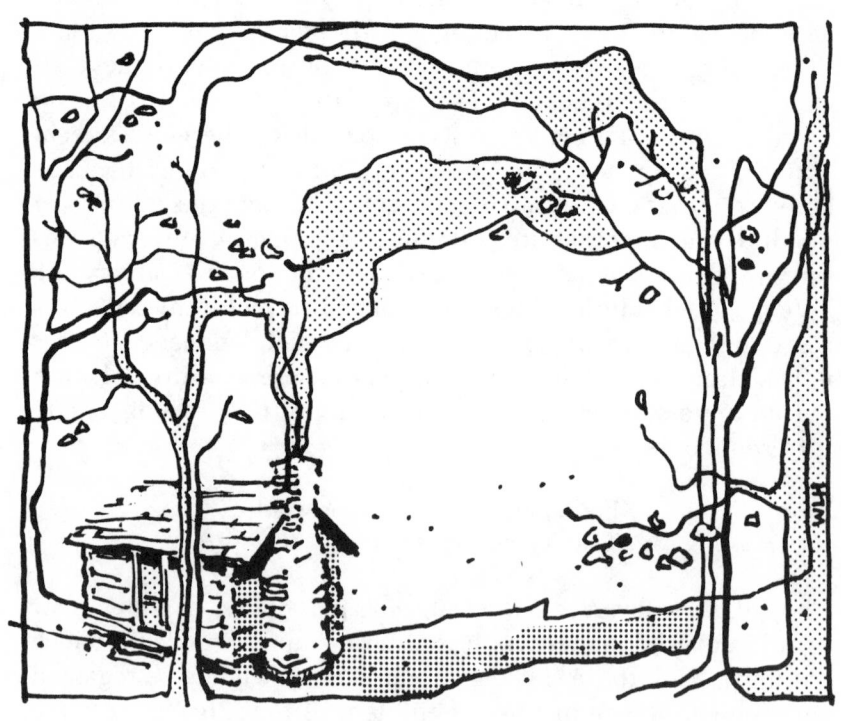

"A CABIN IN THE CLEARING"

Robert Frost's life came full circle. In his final illness he wrote his daughter Lesley from a Boston hospital (12 January 1963): "I am too emotional for my state. Life has been a long trial yet I mean to see more of it." Reading these lines (in Thompson's *Selected Letters*), we might be led to take his use of "trial" lightly— in its reduced colloquial sense. But Lesley, and others close to Frost, understood the religious implications of the remark. From his early years he had regarded life as a mortal trial, a test of man's soul. His father's death came when Rob was just eleven, and the family, left with little money, returned from San Francisco to his father's people in New England. Thompson's biography relates how, in the spring of 1892, young Rob—eighteen—had a mystical experience. In a flash of second sight, as he walked alone on his way to high school, he saw that private, personal sorrow is part of a metaphysical design. He suddenly felt that in some prior plane of existence our souls must heroically choose to be tested by the ordeal of life on earth. And, for the test to be valid, the soul must surrender any memory of having chosen to be tested. This tendency to reconcile divine necessity and human freedom found subsequent expression in Frost's verse as a decree from God:

> "But the pure fate to which you go
> Admits no memory of choice,
> Or the woe were not earthly woe
> To which you give the assenting voice."

That Damascus-like road to school inspired these lines, but it was not until 1906—on the Derry Farm in New Hampshire—that they were born. Quite distinct from Frost's later colloquial poems, "The Trial by Existence" echoes the sublimity of the nineteenth-century poetry that had nurtured him (he confessed a resemblance to Rossetti's "The Blessed Damozel"):

> Even the bravest that are slain
> Shall not dissemble their surprise
> On waking to find valor reign,
> Even as on earth, in paradise;
> And where they sought without the sword
> Wide fields of asphodel fore'er,

> To find that the utmost reward
>   Of daring should be still to dare.
>
> The light of heaven falls whole and white
>   And is not shattered into dyes,
> The light forever is morning light;
>   The hills are verdured pasture-wise;
> The angel hosts with freshness go,
>   And seek with laughter what to brave;—
> And binding all is the hushed snow
>   Of the far-distant breaking wave.

Sergeant's biography of Frost, taking "The Trial by Existence" for its title, tells us that he never read the poem in public. Perhaps he feared that listeners would regard it as mere fantasy. We can guess from Frost's acquaintance with the classics (he slept with copies of Horace and Catullus by his bed) that the poem derives in part from the myth of Er in the tenth book of Plato's *Republic*. It carries nonetheless a feeling of conviction that is largely subdued in his poetry. Here, though he gives his lines the cloak of myth, he speaks unequivocally about the destiny of the soul.

Elsewhere, as we fit together the pieces, a picture of earth as trial ground emerges. We glimpse it through the glass of wit in *A Masque of Reason*, where God explains to Job in modern times,

> Too long I've owed you this apology
> For the apparently unmeaning sorrow
> You were afflicted with in those old days.
> But it was of the essence of the trial
> You shouldn't understand it at the time.
> It had to seem unmeaning to have meaning.

And, later on, Job's wife adds,

> Job says there's no such thing as Earth's becoming
> An easier place for man to save his soul in.
> Except as a hard place to save his soul in,
> A trial ground where he can try himself
> And find out whether he is any good,
> It would be meaningless. It might as well
> Be Heaven at once and have it over with.

A Masque of Reason, like "Kitty Hawk", posits a universe which is God's ongoing experiment, rather than finished creation. Human collaboration is needed to justify God's risk of spirit in material form. God wryly concedes to Job,

> You would have supposed
> One who in the beginning *was* the Word
> Would be in a position to command it.
> I have to wait for words like anyone.

God thanks Job for "releasing [Him]/ From moral bondage to the human race."

> The only free will there at first was man's,
> Who could do good or evil as he chose.
> I had no choice but I must follow him
> With forfeits and rewards he understood—
> Unless I liked to suffer loss of worship.
> I had to prosper good and punish evil.
> You changed all that. You set me free to reign.

Man is given the starring performance in God's creative action, but the Devil has a role, too. His is the "originality," God says, of "invent[ing] Hell." "As for the earth," He continues (speaking still of the Devil), "we groped that out together"—just as, "together," God and Job "Found out the discipline man needed most/ Was to learn his submission to unreason." God speculates,

> Society can never think things out:
> It has to see them acted out by actors,
> Devoted actors at a sacrifice—
> The ablest actors I can lay my hands on.

The drama metaphor is accurate, so long as we remember that the script is not written out in advance. Life is no scenario rolled up on a reel for future display. Men retain free choice and "God must await events/ As well as words." Frost's earth is a stage where a perpetual *happening* is going on—where not only man is on trial, but the spirit of love is tried out, *essayed* as in "Too Anxious for Rivers":

Time was we were molten, time was we were vapor.
What set us on fire and what set us revolving
Lucretius the Epicurean might tell us
'Twas something we knew all about to begin with
And needn't have fared into space like his master
To find 'twas the effort, the essay of love.

"The Trial by Existence" is a neglected but seminal poem. Its premise, "The obscuration upon earth," is an idea Frost held recurrently. Even "A Cabin in the Clearing"—a half-century later— is suffused in murkiness; the "sleepers" lie shrouded in "Smoke," ringed by the "Mist" of mystery. By inversion, the obscuration metaphor yields *clarifications* as well. "Accumulated fact/ Will [not] of itself take fire and light the world up," but—as "Mist" says of the "bewildered" pair in the darkened house—"Putting the lamp out has not put their thought out."

Frost (we noted in Chapter VI) rejected an inclination to call his last book *The Great Misgiving*, and chose as title, *In the Clearing*—evoking memories of his starlit nights and cleared woodlands, of the clean brook water in "Directive"; and the "pasture spring" where (*North of Boston*) he "stop[ped] to rake the leaves away."

(And wait to watch the water clear, I may)

That intention—underplayed by parentheses in "The Pasture"—is a full promise, we find in retrospect, of all Frost was to write. He inscribed the line, with parentheses removed, under the title of *In the Clearing*. Clarity had been his lifelong goal.

When we reach Frost's final *Clearing*, along with him, we have "come too," as he gently bids us in "The Pasture," by *looking*, by *seeing* into things, and—especially—by *watching*. "I could be worse employed," he declares in one of the *Five Nocturnes* ("On Making Certain Anything Has Happened"),

Than as watcher of the void
Whose part should be to tell
What star if any fell.

*   *

> To make sure what star I missed
> I should have to check on my list
> Every star in sight.
> It might take me all night.

According to Thompson's biography, Elinor Frost wrote a friend in 1935 that "about 1890" Robert "got a telescope through the Youth's Companion. He has been astronomical ever since." Literally and figuratively, Frost was always "out for stars" ("Come In"). While sometimes the heavens, like Minerva's "marble eyes" in "Stars," seemed blind to his searching gaze, he tirelessly trusted his poetic talent as a "gift of sight"—as a lens for looking at life, a window for keeping watch. On nights when "the weather [was] clear," the stars, "brought out bright" ("Voice Ways"), seemed to answer his vigil. Such nights inspired a sense of cosmic harmony ("I Will Sing You One-O"), a jubilant feeling of rapport with his friend Sirius, the dog star ("Canis Major"):

> I'm a poor underdog,
> But tonight I will bark
> With the great Overdog
> That romps through the dark.

Human vision, Frost knew, is limited. To shift the metaphor from star-gazing to sea-watching ("Neither Out Far Nor In Deep"), "The people along the sand" cannot see a great distance across the ocean, and their visual probing of its depths is hindered by surface glare. (The reflected "gull" functions like the mirrored image in the well in "For Once, Then, Something.") But they maintain vigilance; "They look at the sea all day."

> They cannot look out far.
> They cannot look in deep.
> But when was that ever a bar
> To any watch they keep?

"Keeping watch" is a constant symbol of Frost's attitude as poet. To express his dedication to poetry he draws also, metaphorically, from the real estate trade. In the *ars poetica* piece "Beech" he stakes a claim to "truth." The Witness Tree is

"impressed"—literally, notched; figuratively, drafted into service—
to testify to a region of certitude within a world of "dark and
doubt." A sacrificial symbol ("deeply wounded"), it is "made [to]
commit to memory" its surrogate role of moral *commit*ment to
defining an area of the mind where, for the moment, we can
"make snug in the limitless"—a phrase Frost used to describe Robinson Crusoe's island and Thoreau's Walden retreat.

Just after "Beech" (*A Witness Tree*, 1942) appears a short verse
which, Frost notes, is quoted from *The New England Primer*.
Titled "Sycamore," it suggests a naive, uncritical acceptance of
Scripture, and by contrast heightens the precariousness of the
"imaginary line" in "Beech" that is traced by the as-if of metaphor.

Gaining possession through sacrifice is the theme of "Beech," as
it is of "The Gift Outright"; there, too, we encounter an allusion to
real estate ("The deed of gift was many deeds of war"). While
"Beech" does not speak explicitly of "deeds," by implication it
enlarges our understanding of Frost's definition of poetry: "words
that have become deeds." In Chapter VI we saw that a poem is no
mere verbal pattern; it is a symbolic *act*. We may guess from the
witness tree figure in "Beech" that a poem is a "deed" in the sense
of *title*, as well, entitling us to a metaphoric clearing on the verge
of dark metaphysical woods.

Frost spent his life pushing the forest back from the ground he
momentarily cleared. He was aware, however, that the wilderness
threatens always to reclaim a "meadow" after men have tamed it
("The Last Mowing"): when the mowers cease their labors, "trees,
seeing the opening,/ March into a shadowy claim." His final volume enabled him to fulfill a prophecy from "Into My Own" in his
first, to "steal away" to the "vastness" of woods. He held up mailing *In the Clearing* to his publishers while he wrote his last poem,
where he "shoulder[s] axe/ . . . in the afterglow" and moves
"Against the trees." Lesley tells me that her father thought about
giving the poem a title—"it would [also] have been the name of
the book." In the end he delivered the lines untitled, a rare act for
him. Was he *releasing title* to earthly goods?

> I link a line of shadowy tracks
> Across the tinted snow.

I believe that in those tracks we can read his parting signature, a quitclaim to his metaphoric clearing. He seemed ready to yield to "the outer dark" that in "Away!" he had playfully resisted.

Undeterred by darkness, Frost had many times stopped by woods and ventured in. The most terrifying of these imaginative trips takes place in the dead of night. "The Draft Horse," grim companion to "Stopping by Woods" (1923), was not published until 1962, but it was written, according to Frost, about 1920. It is an acquiescence to whatever life may bring, like the poem "Acceptance." In "Acceptance," though, nightfall induces a feeling of security; the "pitch-dark limitless grove" of "The Draft Horse" is a setting for nightmarish, irrational cruelty. For the couple who drive "In too frail a buggy . . . / Behind too heavy a horse," darkness is absolute. Even their "lantern . . . wouldn't burn." The grove becomes a chamber of horror:

> And a man came out of the trees
> And took our horse by the head
> And reaching back to his ribs
> Deliberately stabbed him dead.
>
> The ponderous beast went down
> With a crack of a broken shaft.
> And the night drew through the trees
> In one long invidious draft.

The night wind is filled with hate; the killing is brutal and apparently unprovoked. Yet it is interpreted as "deliberate." It is "assumed" by this "most unquestioning pair/ That ever accepted fate" to have some undisclosed purpose. The end of the poem finds them not bitter—just resigned:

> We assumed that the man himself
> Or someone he had to obey
> Wanted us to get down
> And walk the rest of the way.

Here again is the trial-by-existence motif. The couple are latter-day Adam and Eve prototypes (Robert Pack also makes the com-

parison) accepting their human lot without demanding reasons.
They take for granted what Job (*A Masque of Reason*) waited
thousands of years to learn, that "unreason" is a condition of life.
Even so, trusting in some unrevealed design, they invent a rationale for their baffling situation. The unspecified "someone" behind the scene is like a diabolical stage-director artfully manipu-
lating the characters ("ablest actors," God calls all Job-like
figures) to express his own will. But who can say whether he is
diabolical or divine? *A Masque of Reason* gives a clue to his cryptic identity—in the passage where Job comes to see that evil, apparently the work of the Devil, is sanctioned by God:

> The artist in me cries out for design.
> Such devilish ingenuity of torture
> Did seem unlike You, and I tried to think
> The reason might have been some other person's.
> But there is nothing You are not behind.

Similarly, the ordeal of the couple in "The Draft Horse" is perceived as a test. Like Job's trial, it must "seem unmeaning to have
meaning."

Some forty years before it appeared in print, "The Draft
Horse" had explored those dim reaches beyond the *Clearing* in
which Frost staked his last claim. His poems, as he wished, "stick
like burrs." And his log cabin in Ripton, Vermont, stands—like "A
Cabin in the Clearing"—the woods held in check around it.
There, in 1949, he made the confident remark to Selden Rodman,
"I have no religious doubts. Not about God's existence, anyway."[1]
As to an afterlife, Frost is more ambivalent: "the strong are saying
nothing until they see."[2] By "saying nothing" he meant saying nothing *final*. He was content with images and afterimages—and
with leaving the rest "to God."

I've been told a story—first in 1962, and again recently (in more
detail, by William Alfred)— of how Allan Tate once brought
Frost to meet a Jesuit priest. Tate, fresh from his own conversion
to Roman Catholicism, hoped that maybe the author of *A Masque
of Mercy* was ripe for conversion himself. It seemed not, however. As the two turned to leave, Frost asked, "Are you a convert,

Father?" To the good Father's reply that he was not, Frost retorted, "Shake, neither am I!" To be converted, of course, is to *turn* to something different. Frost, as a younger man, had already foretold his own consistency ("Into My Own"):

> They would not find me changed from him they knew—
> Only more sure of all I thought was true.

I think, many times, of Frost's Bread Loaf witticism about doing "good": "I'd rather do *well*." Certainly he knew the value of pride in one's achievement—neatly bundled hay, a finely honed blade, a finished poem. And he knew that a carefully crafted poem can have worth that transcends the private satisfaction felt by its artisan. To strive for clarity in poetic language is, perhaps, ultimately to do *good*. If words are "deeds . . . flat and final like the show-down in poker" (see page 68), then they may be weighed on the scales of morality, not just assayed as art.

Robert Frost took his risks and played out the game. He kept his watch, along with Keeper in the second masque, over a store of books and "bed of world-flowers." Then he moved on. "We are all each other's keepers," he had written Roy Elliott back in 1938. What has this Genesis-inspired altruism to do with writing poetry, an apparently self-indulgent vocation? The answer is that, for Frost, design was *sacred*, and the pursuit of clarification through art was inevitably religious. Once, talking with his friend Elizabeth Sergeant, he gestured toward his thick green volume of the *Complete Poems* on the arm of his beloved Morris chair: "There I rest my case." If there is any verdict beyond that of time and human judgment, I believe his case will stand up well.

Notes

NOTES TO PREFACE

1. Lionel Trilling, "A Speech on Robert Frost: A Cultural Episode," *Partisan Review*, XXVI (Summer 1959), 445–52.

2. "Robert Frost and the Dark Woods," *Yale Review*, XXIII (March 1934), 514–20.

3. Hyde Cox and Edward Connery Lathem, eds., *Selected Prose of Robert Frost* (New York, 1968), p. 18.

4. "Robert Frost: or, the Spiritual Drifter as Poet," *Sewanee Review*, LVI (August 1948), 564–96.

5. *Human Values in the Poetry of Robert Frost* (Durham, N. C., 1960), pp. 37, 184.

6. Jac Tharpe, ed., *Frost: Centennial Essays* III (Jackson, Miss., 1978), p. 281.

7. For a discussion of Thomism in AMOM see William G. O'Donnell, "Parable in Poetry," *Virginia Quarterly Review*, XXV (September 1949), 269–82.

8. Cox and Lathem, eds., *Selected Prose*, p. 24.

9. *Ibid.*, p. 44.

10. *Ibid.*, p. 97.

11. Edward Connery Lathem, ed., *Interviews with Robert Frost* (New York, 1966), p. 149.

12. "The Humanistic Idealism of Robert Frost," *American Literature*, XIII (November 1941), 221. See also *The Heel of Elohim: Science and Values in Modern American Poetry* (Norman, Oklahoma, 1950), where Waggoner devotes a chapter to an assessment of Frost's philosophical position.

13. Frost's fondness for the paradoxical tag "Old Testament Christian" is cited by Victor E. Reichert in "The Faith of Robert Frost," *Frost: Centennial Essays* (Jackson, Miss., 1974), p. 421; and "The Robert Frost I Knew," *Frost: Centennial Essays* III (Jackson, Miss., 1978), p. 114. See also my essay in that volume, "An Old Testament Christian," pp. 316–49.

14. For a discussion of the Bergsonian strain in Frost's poetry see my

125

essay "The Height of Feeling Free: Frost and Bergson," *Texas Quarterly*, XIX (Spring 1976), 128–43. I find that George W. Nitchie's term "incompleteness" (*Human Values in the Poetry of Robert Frost*, p. 185) applied to Frost's artistic vision, can be interpreted quite differently in the light of Bergson's idea of creative evolution.

15. *Fire and Ice* (New York, 1961 edition), p. 177.

16. *Ibid.*, p. 182.

17. "Robert Frost," *Yale Review*, XLIII (December 1953), 205, 212-13.

18. *The Concept of Nature in Nineteenth-Century English Poetry* (New York, 1956), pp. 551-53.

19. Cox and Lathem, eds., *Selected Prose*, pp. 18, 107.

20. *Ibid.*, p. 106.

21. *Ibid.*, p. 106.

22. *Ibid.*, pp. 18-19.

23. Frost's "definition of poetry," quoted in Gorham B. Munson, *Robert Frost: A Study in Sensibility and Good Sense* (Port Washington, N.Y., 1968 edition), p. 98. (Originally published in 1927.)

NOTES TO CHAPTER I

1. See Victor E. Reichert, "The Faith of Robert Frost," *Frost: Centennial Essays* (Jackson, Miss., 1974), p. 418. Rabbi Reichert recalls the "last time" he saw the poet:

It was here in the School House, Ripton [the rabbi's summer residence in Vermont]. Frost had come back from Russia and there was a gathering in our Ripton home. Suddenly, out of nowhere, sitting side by side and chatting, Frost said to me, "Victor, what do you think are the chances of life after death?" I teased Frost by reminding him that when you ask a Jew a question, you don't get an answer; just another question. In the Book of Job, God never answers Job. Instead, God belabors Job with one great question after another. So I said to Robert, "What do you think?" Frost became deeply silent and then he said to me, "With so many ladders going up everywhere, there must be something for them to lean against." I never forgot that poignant remark. Here was Frost,

deep in his eighties, wistful about the prospect ahead. And what an image it suggested of Jacob's ladder with the angels ascending and descending.
What an image, we may also conclude, Frost gave the rabbi, and us all, for extending *further* upward "Toward heaven" his "long two-pointed ladder" of "After Apple-Picking."

2. Edward Connery Lathem, ed., *Interviews with Robert Frost* (New York, 1966), p. 295.

3. "The Agitated Heart," *Atlantic Monthly*, CCXX (July 1967), 72.

NOTES TO CHAPTER II

1. When Frost submitted "A Prayer in Spring" for inclusion in Whit Burnett's 1942 anthology *This is My Best*, he omitted the final stanza. The question of his motivation arises. Artistic considerations could hardly have justified the omission, since the poem is weakened and seems to end in mid air with three stanzas of petition and no conclusion. Perhaps reticence to reveal religious belief led him to the decision. "What lies unvoiced on earth/Is heaven sung" (from RF's "Parting").

2. Evidence that the star is Sirius is contained in Frost's footnote to "One More Brevity" (at line 65):
But see "The Great Overdog" and "Choose Something Like a Star," in which latter the star could hardly have been a planet since fixity is of the essence of the piece.

3. The phrase occurs in Frost's Introduction to Edwin Arlington Robinson's *King Jasper* in a passage where he develops the principle of *correspondence* in art:
Mind must convince mind that it can uncurl and wave the same filaments of subtlety, soul convince soul that it can give off the same shimmers of eternity.

4. See Lawrance Thompson, *Robert Frost: The Early Years* (New York, 1966), pp. 198–200, for an account of the impact upon Frost of Francis Thompson's "The Hound of Heaven" when he first encountered it in the Old Corner Bookshop, Boston, in 1895.

5. Father Arthur MacGillivray of Boston College, a good friend of Frost in the later years, recalls his first meeting with the poet on No-

vember 30, 1950, at the YMHA in New York City. Frost dismissed the long-standing question of his year of birth (1874 or 1875?): "The records of birth were lost in the San Francisco conflagration." He added, for emphasis, "They say 'conflagration,' you know," and went on, "I'm not worried about that. What I *am* worried about is my dog. *He's* getting old." "What's his name?" the priest asked, after a moment. "Gillie—it's a Scotch name meaning a slave, or a servant." To that Father MacGillivray remarked that he had just been reading about his own name which came from "Gillebreagh, meaning a master." "Well, then," Frost concluded positively, "it's just the opposite." (In "One More Brevity," Gillie—transformed as "Gus"—*combines* the roles, as most dogs can, of servant and master.)

NOTES TO CHAPTER III

1. "Frost: Country Poet and Cosmopolitan Poet," *Yale Review*, LIX (Winter 1970), 191.

2. *The Dimensions of Robert Frost* (New York, 1958), p. 162. See also Cook's account of the event in "Robert Frost's Asides on his Poetry," *American Literature*, XIX (January 1948), 357.

3. The typescript, presumably by Frost, was found among the George H. Browne papers now housed at Plymouth State College Library, New Hampshire. It is dated (in GHB? handwriting) "Spring 1920." "A Favour" appeared in *The London Mercury* (December 1920) and "Snow Dust" was published in *Yale Review*, X (January 1921), 258.

4. Radcliffe Squires, *The Major Themes of Robert Frost* (Ann Arbor, Mich., 1963), p. 15 (letter dated 22 May 1915).

5. For an application of Jung's archetypal symbols to artistic imagery, see: Elizabeth Drew, *T. S. Eliot: The Design of His Poetry* (New York, 1949), Chapter X.

6. The Calvinist doctrine of election is suggested also in "The Strong Are Saying Nothing": "The final flat of the hoe's approval stamp/ Is reserved for the bed of a few selected seed." The lines are of considerable interest for their Biblical resonances. The parable of the sower, which Frost admired, is implanted in them. They point as well to an intricate psychological circuitry in Frost's vision. The low-keyed juxta-

position of *reserved* and *selected* indicates an underlying link between two recurring motifs in the poetry: the use of *reserve*—as both subject matter and artistic method—and the conceptual matrix of *favor-grace-mercy*. While the matrix usually takes the beneficent form of unmerited gift, the term *selected*, with its Calvinist overtones, evokes the harsher aspect of the idea, the arbitrariness of reward or punishment.

NOTES TO CHAPTER IV

1. Autograph manuscript notebook containing varying amounts of prose and verse, mostly unpublished. Circa 1950. Currently in Boston University Mugar Library, Special Collections. I have preserved Frost's spelling and punctuation (but not paragraphing, which is difficult to determine) and, of course, combined his interpolations and deletions into a finished text.

2. Daniel Smythe, *Robert Frost Speaks* (New York, 1964), p. 136.

3. Reginald L. Cook, *The Dimensions of Robert Frost* (New York, 1958), p. 149. See also Lawrance Thompson, ed., *Selected Letters of Robert Frost* (New York, 1964), p. 460, where Frost chides his friend Roy Elliott for asserting that "one can no more be religious, outside of the church than one can be patriotic without belonging to a country." Frost adds, parenthetically, "You should have said, without belonging to the army."

NOTES TO CHAPTER V

1. Letter dated 22 September 1970. Thompson wrote in response to a brief conversation we had shortly before at the New England Book Festival and to my mailing him my manuscript article "Robert Frost's 'Grace Notes.' " On the subject of "design" and of Frost's "trickiness" Thompson says:

. . . in what sense was the visible world, for Frost, "the dial plate of the invisible" and in what sense was it not? To answer that adequately . . . you'd have to dig beneath Emerson, into what might be called orthodox Christian doctrine on the notion that the visible is somehow the dial plate of the invisible. You have it in a Christian sense long before Emerson gives it a Transcendental twist. But look at Frost's poem, "A Prayer in Spring." Look at his famous letter to *The Amherst Student* . . . .

. . . while Frost is coy and cagey in his handling of the Christian concept of design—in the sense that the visible aspects of nature do serve as signs-emblems-types to reveal the invisible aspects of God—nevertheless, he subscribes to that orthodox Christian notion. So does Emerson, as a matter of fact.

2. Sidney Hayes Cox, 'The Sincerity of Robert Frost," *New Republic*, XII (25 August 1917), 109.

3. Lawrance Thompson, ed., *Selected Letters of Robert Frost* (New York, 1964), p. 465.

4. *The Pastoral Art of Robert Frost* (New Haven, 1960), p. 97. See also p. 91, n. 9, for a quotation from Frost's letter to Norman Holmes Pearson:

If you had permitted me one nomination it might have been "The Grindstone," a favorite of mine and to me "an image of the naughty world." You know Herschel had a grindstone theory of the universe.

Lynen notes, on Pearson's advising, that the image of the grindstone as a metaphor for the world did not originate with Sir William Herschel, but with Simon Newcomb a century later (c. 1908) in discussing Herschel's theory of the shape of the universe. Frost's phrase "naughty world" means, I think, "naughty mankind," in the context of the Biblical myth of the Fall.

NOTES TO CHAPTER VI

1. See Theodore Morrison, "The Agitated Heart," *Atlantic Monthly*, CCXX (July 1967), 78. Morrison records the gist of Hyde Cox's notes of a conversation with Frost prior to 1947 when *Steeple Bush* was published. (*Steeple Bush* includes "Directive," which initially appeared in 1946.) The poet was delighted with Cox's apprising him that, according to

Saint Matthew and Saint Mark, Christ spoke in parables to make it harder, not as is generally thought easier, to understand Him. "R. F. pointed out that it is the same as for poetry; only those who approach it in the right way can understand it. And not everyone can understand no matter what they do because it just isn't in them. They cannot 'be saved.' . . . And R. F. quickly connected this quotation with the thought that unless you come to the subject of poetry 'as a child' you cannot hope to enter into 'the kingdom of heaven.' " Cox recalls that, "From this evening on, the quotation from St. Mark . . . began to appear in R. F.'s conversation and . . . in his public talks." Morrison also bears testimony to the fact.

2. John Ciardi, "Robert Frost: Master Conversationalist at Work," *Saturday Review*, XLII (21 March 1959), 17.

3. Frost's "definition of poetry," quoted in Gorham B. Munson, *Robert Frost: A Study in Sensibility and Good Sense* (Port Washington, N.Y., 1968 edition), pp. 97-98. (Originally published in 1927.)

4. See George W. Nitchie, *Human Values in the Poetry of Robert Frost* (Durham, N. C., 1960), p. 211:

Yeats committed himself to his laborious play, developed a coherent if absurd theory of reality, and wrote great poems. Frost has not made that mortal commitment; we can never really accept or reject his vision of reality, because it is never quite clear, never quite coherent, never quite there.

See also my response to Nitchie's charge of Frost's "incompleteness" (*Ibid.*, p. 185) in "The Height of Feeling Free: Frost and Bergson," *Texas Quarterly*, XIX (Spring 1976), 128–43.

5. I am indebted to Professor Gerald Fitzgerald, Boston University, for my information about the Petrarchan sonnet and its variations.

6. Phrase suggested to me by Professor Fitzgerald.

NOTES TO CHAPTER VII

1. *Errand Into the Wilderness* (New York, 1964; originally Cambridge, Mass., 1956), p. 185. For an in-depth consideration of the continuity "From Edwards to Emerson" see entire Chapter VIII.

2. Mason I. Lowance, Jr., "Images or Shadows of Divine Things:

The Typology of Jonathan Edwards," *Early American Literature*, V (Spring 1970), 177.

3. Edward Connery Lathem, ed., *Interviews with Robert Frost* (New York, 1966), p. 49.

4. Reginald L. Cook, "Emerson and Frost: A Parallel of Seers," *New England Quarterly*, XXXI (June 1958), 205.

5. Mark Harris, "Old Enough to Know, Young Enough to Care," *Life*, LI (1 December 1961), 122.

6. Lawrance Thompson, *Robert Frost: The Years of Triumph* (New York, 1970), p. 693, n. 23.

7. *Ibid.*, p. 693, n. 23.

NOTES TO CHAPTER VIII

1. Frost's use of "as if" ("West-Running Brook"; "Two Look at Two") is partly a rhetorical device for evading definitive statement. But beneath the verbal strategy lies a fundamental artistic principle, suggested in his Introduction to Edwin Arlington Robinson's *King Jasper*. There he quotes admiringly the ending of Robinson's "The Dark Hills" —"As if the last of days/ Were fading and all wars were done"—and comments:

Give us immedicable woes—woes that nothing can be done for— woes flat and final. And then to play. The play's the thing. Play's the thing. All virtue in "as if."

The passage recognizes the transforming power of man's imagination in its encounter with immutable physical fact. The metaphoric "as if" is called a *virtue*, a term that implies both goodness and (from its Latin root) manliness, courage. Frost saw the power of play as a courageous way of confronting human "griefs," which are irrevocable, incurable. ("Griefs are a form of patience," quite the opposite of "grievances," which he did not like and which he thought should perhaps be "restricted to prose.")

2. The uncompromising realism and non-sentimentality expressed in "The Need of Being Versed in Country Things" should not be invoked to deny the potential of a spiritually symbolic universe in "Two Look at Two," a poem which is given its energy by a visionary impulse.

NOTES TO CHAPTER IX

1. Mark Harris, "Old Enough to Know, Young Enough to Care," *Life*, LI (1 December 1961), 122. Frost explained, "You're always believing ahead of your evidence. . . . The most creative thing in us is to believe a thing in, in love, in all else." To believe something *in* (as opposed to *believing in* something) is to engage actively in the process of belief, not to be a passive recipient. Frost's consistency in this attitude becomes evident if we turn to his remarks thirty years earlier ("Education by Poetry"): ". . . the belief in God is a relationship you enter into with Him to bring about the future." He named the "two or three places where we know belief outside of religion"—"the self-belief, the love-belief, and the art-belief"; all, he said, are "closely related to the God-belief."

2. Theodore Morrison, "The Agitated Heart," *Atlantic Monthly*, CCXX (July 1967), 79.

3. See John Robert Doyle, Jr., "A Reading of Frost's 'Directive,' " *Georgia Review*, XXII (Winter 1968), 501-08. After connecting "whole" and "holy" through their common Old English root *halig*, from *hal* (recall my Chapter VI), Doyle uses the relationship to identify the Biblical "directive" that Frost very likely had in mind when he wrote "Drink and be whole again beyond confusion":

> Frost's studies at this time must surely have apprised him of the pivotal injunction of the Old Testament, . . . that man's true purpose on earth is to become "holy." . . . "Ye shall be holy: for I the Lord your God am holy."

NOTES TO CHAPTER X

1. *Tongues of Fallen Angels* (New York, 1974), p. 41. Frost's assertion of belief was his counterpunch to Rodman's question about "The Bear"—whether the poem "implies a sly criticism of preachers." "Could be," Frost replied, "I despise religiosity." He habitually distinguished between belonging to a church and *being religious*. Recall his jibe at T. S. Eliot: "Eliot's a churchman; *I'm* religious."

2. See my comment on the implicit Calvinism in "The Strong Are Saying Nothing" (Chapter III, n. 6). Frost's religious stoicism is reflected in this poem and in a comment he made at Bread Loaf, Vermont, on 26 August 1961, after reading aloud "Provide, Provide": "The worst part of life is the end. You can't keep the end from being hard, not the state—nobody but God."

Selected Bibliography

I. *PRIMARY MATERIAL*: Essays, Letters, Interviews

Anderson, Margaret B. *Robert Frost and John Bartlett: The Record of a Friendship* (New York, 1963).

Cox, Hyde and Edward Connery Lathem, eds. *Selected Prose of Robert Frost* (New York, 1966).

Evans, William R. *Robert Frost and Sidney Cox: Forty Years of Friendship* (Hanover, N. H., 1981).

Grade, Arnold, ed. *Family Letters of Robert and Elinor Frost* (Albany, N. Y., 1972).

Hall, Donald. "Vanity, Fame, Love, and Robert Frost," *Remembering Poets: Reminiscences and Opinions* (New York, 1977).

Harris, Mark. "Old Enough to Know, Young Enough to Care," *Life* 51 (1 December 1961).

Lathem, Edward Connery, ed. *Interviews with Robert Frost* (New York, 1966).

Rodman, Selden. "Robert Frost," *Tongues of Fallen Angels* (New York, 1974).

Thompson, Lawrance, ed. *Selected Letters of Robert Frost* (New York, 1964).

Untermeyer, Louis, ed. *Letters of Robert Frost to Louis Untermeyer* (New York, 1963).

II. *SECONDARY MATERIAL*: Bibliography, Biography, Criticism

A. *Books*

Barry, Elaine. *Robert Frost* (New York, 1973).

135

Brower, Reuben. *The Poetry of Robert Frost: Constellations of Intention* (New York, 1963).

Cook, Reginald L. *The Dimensions of Robert Frost* (New York, 1958).

————. *Robert Frost: A Living Voice* (Amherst, Mass., 1974).

Cox, James M., ed. *Robert Frost: A Collection of Critical Essays* (Englewood Cliffs, N. J., 1962).

Cox, Sidney. *Robert Frost: Original "Ordinary" Man* (New York, 1929).

————. *A Swinger of Birches: A Portrait of Robert Frost* (New York, 1957).

Doyle, John R., Jr. *The Poetry of Robert Frost: An Analysis* (Johannesburg, S. A., 1962; New York, 1973).

Francis, Robert. *Frost: A Time to Talk* (Amherst, Mass., 1972).

Frost, Lesley. *New Hampshire's Child: The Derry Journals of Lesley Frost* (Albany, N. Y., 1969).

Gerber, Philip L. *Robert Frost* (Twayne United States Authors Series, New York, 1966).

Gould, Jean. *Robert Frost: The Aim Was Song* (New York, 1964).

Greenleaf, Robert K. *Robert Frost's "Directive" and the Spiritual Journey* (privately printed by The Nimrod Press, Boston, 1963).

Greiner, Donald J. *A Guide to Robert Frost* (Columbus, Ohio, 1969; pamphlet).

————. *Robert Frost: The Poet and His Critics* (Chicago, 1974).

Harris, Kathryn Gibbs, ed. *Robert Frost: Studies of the Poetry* (Boston, 1979).

Isaacs, Elizabeth, *An Introduction to Robert Frost* (Denver, 1962).

Kemp, John C. *Robert Frost and New England: The Poet as Regionalist* (Princeton, N. J., 1979).

Kuzma, Greg, ed. *Gone Into If Not Explained: Essays on Poems by Robert Frost* (*Pebble* mag. #s 14 & 15, Crete, Neb., 1976).

Lathem, Edward Connery, ed. *A Concordance to the Poetry of Robert Frost* (New York, 1971).

Lentricchia, Frank. *Robert Frost: Modern Poetics and the Landscapes of Self* (Durham, N. C., 1975).

_____and Lentricchia, Melissa Christensen. *Robert Frost: A Bibliography, 1913–1974* (Metuchen, N. J., 1976).

Lynen, John F. *The Pastoral Art of Robert Frost* (New Haven, 1960).

Mertins, Louis. *Robert Frost, Life and Talks-Walking* (Norman, Okla., 1965).

Morrison, Kathleen. *Robert Frost: A Pictorial Chronicle* (New York, 1974).

Munson, Gorham B. *Robert Frost: A Study in Sensibility and Good Sense* (New York, 1927; reissued 1968).

Nitchie, George W. *Human Values in the Poetry of Robert Frost: A Study of a Poet's Convictions* (Durham, N. C., 1960).

Poirier, Richard. *Robert Frost: The Work of Knowing* (New York, 1977).

Potter, James L. *Robert Frost Handbook* (Pennsylvania State University Park, 1980).

Sergeant, Elizabeth Shepley. *Robert Frost: The Trial by Existence* (New York, 1960).

Simpson, Lewis P. *Profile of Robert Frost* (Merrill Profiles Series, Columbus, Ohio, 1971).

Smythe, Daniel. *Robert Frost Speaks* (New York, 1964).

Squires, Radcliffe. *The Major Themes of Robert Frost* (Ann Arbor, Mich., 1963).

Sutton, William A., ed. *Newdick's Season of Frost: An Interrupted Biography of Robert Frost* (Albany, N. Y., 1976).

Tharpe, Jac L., ed. *Frost: Centennial Essays*, 3 vols. (Jackson, Miss., 1974; 1976; 1978).

Thompson, Lawrance. *Emerson and Frost: Critics of Their Times* (Philo-Biblon Club, Philadelphia, 1940).

_____. *Fire and Ice: The Art and Thought of Robert Frost* (New York, 1942).

_____.*Robert Frost* (Univ. of Minn. Pamphlets on American Writers, #2, Minneapolis, 1960).

_____. *Robert Frost: The Early Years*, 1874–1915 (New York, 1966).

_____. *Robert Frost: The Years of Triumph*, 1915–1938 (New York, 1970).

_____and Winnick, R. H. *Robert Frost: The Later Years*, 1938–1963 (New York, 1976).

Thornton, Richard, ed. *Recognition of Robert Frost: Twenty-Fifth Anniversary* (New York, 1937).

Van Egmond, Peter, ed. *The Critical Reception of Robert Frost* (Boston, 1974).

B.   *Articles*

Bacon, Helen. "In- and Outdoor Schooling: Robert Frost and the Classics," *American Scholar* 43 (Fall 1974) 640-49.

Bartini, Arnold G. "Robert Frost and Moral Neutrality," *CEA Critic* 38 (January 1976) 22–24.

Beach, Joseph Warren. "Robert Frost," *Yale Review* 43 (December 1953) 204–17.

Bieganowski, Ronald. "Sense of Place and Religious Consciousness," *Robert Frost: Studies of the Poetry*, ed. Kathryn Gibbs Harris (Boston, 1979) pp. 29–47.

Blum, Margaret M. "Robert Frost's 'Directive': A Theological Reading," *Modern Language Notes* 76 (June 1961) 524–25.

Boroff, Marie. "Robert Frost's New Testament: Language and the Poem," *Modern Philology* 69 (August 1971) 36–56.

Bort, Barry D. "Frost and the Deeper Vision," *Midwest Quarterly* 5 (Fall 1963) 59–67.

Ciardi, John. "Robert Frost: Master Conversationalist at Work," *Saturday Review* 42 (21 March 1959) 17–20, 54.

Clark, David R. "An Excursion upon the Criticism of Robert Frost's 'Directive,' " *Costerus: Essays in English and American Language and Literature* 8 (1973) 3–56.

Coale, Samuel. "The Emblematic Encounter of Robert Frost," *Frost: Centennial Essays*, ed. Jac L. Tharpe (Jackson, Miss., 1974) pp. 89–107.

Cook, Marjorie. "Detachment, Irony, and Commitment," *Robert Frost: Studies of the Poetry*, ed. Kathryn Gibbs Harris (Boston, 1979) pp. 49–62.

Cook, Reginald L. "Emerson and Frost: A Parallel of Seers," *New England Quarterly* 31 (June 1958) 200–217.

————. "A Parallel of Parablists: Thoreau and Frost," *The Thoreau Centennial*, ed. Walter Harding (Albany, N. Y., 1964) pp. 65–79.

————. "Robert Frost's Constellated Sky," *Western Humanities Review* 22 (Summer 1968) 189–98.

————. "Robert Frost: An Equilibrist's Field of Vision," *Massachusetts Review* 15 (Summer 1974) 385–401.

Cox, James M. "Robert Frost and the Edge of the Clearing," *Virginia Quarterly Review* 35 (Winter 1959) 73–88.

Dabbs, J. McBride. "Robert Frost and the Dark Woods," *Yale Review* 23 (March 1934) 514–20.

Donoghue, Denis. "Robert Frost," *Connoisseurs of Chaos* (New York, 1965) pp. 160–89.

Dougherty, James P. "Robert Frost's 'Directive' to the Wilderness," *American Quarterly* 18 (Summer 1966) 209–19.

Doyle, John Robert, Jr. "A Reading of Robert Frost's 'Directive,' " *Georgia Review* 22 (Winter 1968) 501–8.

Duvall, S. P. C. "Robert Frost's 'Directive' Out of Walden," *American Literature* 31 (January 1960) 482–88.

Elkins, William J. "The Spiritual Crisis in 'Stopping by Woods,' " *Cresset* 35 (February 1972) 6–8.

Ferguson, Alfred R. "Frost and the Paradox of the Fortunate Fall," *Frost: Centennial Essays*, ed. Jac L. Tharpe (Jackson, Miss., 1974) pp. 427–40.

Fleissner, Robert F. "Like 'Pythagoras' Comparison of the Universe with Number': A Frost-Tennyson Correlation," *Frost: Centennial Essays*, ed. Jac L. Tharpe (Jackson, Miss., 1974) pp. 207–20.

Hall, Dorothy Judd. "Reserve in the Art of Robert Frost," *Texas Quarterly* 6 (Summer 1963) 60–67. (Published under the name Dorothy Judd.)

———. "Painterly Qualities in Frost's Lyric Poetry," *Ball State University Forum* 11 (Winter 1970) 9–13.

———. "The Height of Feeling Free: Frost and Bergson," *Texas Quarterly* 19 (Spring 1976) 128–43.

———. "An Old Testament Christian," *Frost: Centennial Essays* III, ed. Jac L. Tharpe (Jackson, Miss., 1978) pp. 316–49.

Jones, Howard Mumford. "The Cosmic Loneliness of Robert Frost," *Belief and Disbelief in American Literature* (Chicago, 1967) pp. 116–42.

Juhnke, Anna K. "Religion in Robert Frost's Poetry: The Play for Self-Possession," *American Literature* 36 (May 1964) 153–64.

Kau, Joseph. " 'Trust . . . to go by contraries': Incarnation and the Paradox of Belief in the Poetry of Frost," *Frost: Centennial Essays* II, ed. Jac L. Tharpe (Jackson, Miss., 1976) pp. 99–111.

Knox, George. "A Backward Motion Toward the Source," *Personalist* 47 (Summer 1966) 365–81.

McClanahan, Thomas. "Frost's Theodicy: 'Word I Had No One Left But God,' " *Frost: Centennial Essays* II, ed. Jac L. Tharpe (Jackson, Miss., 1976) pp. 112–26.

Montgomery, Marion. "Robert Frost and His Use of Barriers: Man vs. Nature toward God," *South Atlantic Quarterly* 57 (Summer 1958) 339–353; reprinted in *Robert Frost: A Collection of Critical Essays*, ed. James M. Cox (Englewood Cliffs, N. J., 1962) pp. 138–50.

Morrison, Theodore. "The Agitated Heart," *Atlantic Monthly* 220 (July 1967) 72–79.

———. "Frost: Country Poet and Cosmopolitan Poet," *Yale Review* 59 (Winter 1970) 179–96.

Morse, Stearns. "The Wholeness of Robert Frost," *Virginia Quarterly Review* 19 (Summer 1943) 412–16.

Mulder, William. "Seeing 'New Englandly': Planes of Perception in Emily Dickinson and Robert Frost," *New England Quarterly* 52 (December 1979) 550-59.

Nitchie, George W. "A Momentary Stay Against Confusion," *Robert Frost: A Collection of Critical Essays*, ed. James M. Cox (Englewood Cliffs, N. J., 1962) pp. 159–76.

O'Donnell, William G. "Parable in Poetry," *Virginia Quarterly Review* 25 (Spring 1949) 269–82.

Ogilvie, John T. "From Woods to Stars: A Pattern of Imagery in Robert Frost's Poetry," *South Atlantic Quarterly* 58 (Winter 1959) 64–76.

Pack, Robert. "Robert Frost's 'Enigmatical Reserve': The Poet as Teacher and Preacher," *Robert Frost: Lectures on the Centennial of His Birth* (Library of Congress, Washington, 1975) pp. 43–55.

Perrine, Laurence. "Robert Frost and the Idea of Immortality," *Frost: Centennial Essays* II, ed. Jac L. Tharpe (Jackson, Miss., 1976) pp. 85–98.

Peters, Robert. "The Truth of Frost's 'Directive,' " *Modern Language Notes* 75 (January 1960) 29–32.

Rechnitz, Robert M. "The Tragic Vision of Robert Frost," *Frost: Centennial Essays*, ed. Jac L. Tharpe (Jackson, Miss., 1974) pp. 133–46.

Reichert, Victor E. "The Faith of Robert Frost," *Frost: Centennial Essays*, ed. Jac L. Tharpe (Jackson, Miss., 1974) pp. 415–26.

———. "The Robert Frost I Knew," *Frost: Centennial Essays* III, ed. Jac L. Tharpe (Jackson, Miss., 1978) pp. 105–22.

Ryan, Alvan S. "Frost and Emerson: Voice and Vision," *Profile of Robert Frost*, ed. Lewis P. Simpson (Columbus, Ohio, 1971) pp. 51–65.

Sister Catherine Theresa. "New Testament Interpretations of Robert Frost's Poems," *Ball State University Forum* 11 (Winter 1970) 50–54.

Stanlis, Peter J. "Robert Frost's Masques and the Classic American Tradition," *Frost: Centennial Essays*, ed. Jac L. Tharpe (Jackson, Miss., 1974) pp. 441–68.

———. "Acceptable in Heaven's Sight," *Frost: Centennial Essays* III, ed. Jac L. Tharpe (Jackson, Miss., 1978) pp. 179–311.

Thompson, Lawrance. "A Native to the Grain of the American Idiom," *Saturday Review* 42 (21 March 1959) 21, 55–56.

Trilling, Lionel. "A Speech on Robert Frost: A Cultural Episode," *Partisan Review* 26 (Summer 1959) 445–52; reprinted in *Robert Frost: A*

Collection of Critical Essays, ed. James M. Cox (Englewood Cliffs, N. J., 1962) pp. 151–58.

Van Dore, Wade. "I'd Rather Believe in Inspiration," *Yankee* 35 (November 1971) 116–19, 204, 207.

————. "In Robert Frost's Rubbers," *Michigan Quarterly Review* 11 (Spring 1972) 122–26.

Waggoner, Hyatt Howe. "The Humanistic Idealism of Robert Frost," *American Literature* 13 (November 1941) 207–23.

Warner, Stephen D. "Robert Frost in the Clearing: The Risk of Spirit in Substantiation," *Frost: Centennial Essays*, ed. Jac L. Tharpe (Jackson, Miss., 1974) pp. 398–411.

Water, Gregory. " 'Directive': Frost's Magical Mystery Tour," *Concerning Poetry* 9 (Spring 1976) 33–38.

Watkins, Floyd C. "Going and Coming Back: Robert Frost's Religious Poetry," *South Atlantic Quarterly* 73 (Autumn 1974) 445–59.

Watts, Harold H. "Robert Frost and the Interrupted Dialogue," *American Literature* 27 (March 1955) 69–87; reprinted in *Robert Frost: A Collection of Critical Essays*, ed. James M. Cox (Englewood Cliffs, N. J., 1962) pp. 105–22.

Winters, Yvor. "Robert Frost: or, the Spiritual Drifter as Poet," *Sewanee Review* 56 (Autumn 1948) 564–96; reprinted in *Robert Frost: A Collection of Critical Essays*, ed. James M. Cox (Englewood Cliffs, N. J., 1962) pp. 58–82.

III. BACKGROUND SOURCES

Bergson, Henri. Creative Evolution (New York, 1911) authorized translation by Arthur Mitchell.

Brumm, Ursula. *American Thought and Religious Typology* (New Brunswick, N. J., 1970) translated from the 1963 German edition by John Hoaglund.

Burrows, Millar. *An Outline of Biblical Theology* (Philadelphia, 1946).

Emerson, Edward Waldo, ed. *Nature, Addresses and Lectures by Ralph Waldo Emerson* (Boston, 1903).

Emerson, Ralph Waldo. *Prose Works* (Boston, 1870).

————. *The Complete Works of Ralph Waldo Emerson* (Boston, 1876).

Fosdick, Harry Emerson. *A Guide to Understanding the Bible: The Development of Ideas Within the Old and New Testaments* (New York, 1938).

Henry, Carl F. H., ed. *Basic Christian Doctrines* (New York, 1962).

James, William. *The Will to Believe and Other Essays in Popular Philosophy* (New York, 1897).

————. *A Pluralistic Universe* (New York, 1920).

Landis, Benson Y. *An Outline of the Bible Book by Book* (New York, 1963).

Lowance, Mason I., Jr. "Images or Shadows of Divine Things: the Typology of Jonathan Edwards," *Early American Literature* 5 (Spring 1970) 141–81.

Miller, Perry. *Errand into the Wilderness* (Cambridge, Mass., 1956; reprinted New York, 1964).

Stanford, Donald E., ed. *The Poems of Edward Taylor* (New Haven, 1960).

Walvoord, John F., ed. *Inspiration and Interpretation* (Grand Rapids, Mich., 1957).

Index

PROPER NAMES OF INDIVIDUALS; PHILOSOPHICAL OR RELIGIOUS CATEGORIES

Alfred, William, 122
Auden, W. H. xv

Bacon, Helen 109
Beach, Joseph Warren xxi–xxii, 79
Beckett, Samuel xv
Bergson, Henri xiii, xxi, xxv, 51–52, 54, 58, 65, 74, 89–92, 96
Blake, William 84, 96
Blum, Margaret 109
Brower, Reuben 81, 107, 110
Browning, Robert 103

Calvinism 35, 75–77
Christ/Christianity xx–xxi, 23, 37, 38, 41–42, 49, 52, 65, 71, 75, 106–07, 109–110, 113, 130–31
Ciardi, John 131
Cook, Reginald L. 28–29, 129, 132
Cox, Hyde 109–10, 125, 126, 130–31
Cox, Sidney Hayes 7, 8, 46, 53, 130

Dabbs, J. McBride xvi, 1, 11
DeVoto, Bernard 5
Dickinson, Emily 3, 32
Doyle, John Robert xi, 106–07, 133
Drew, Elizabeth 128

Edwards, Jonathan 76–77
Eliot, T. S. xv, xvi, 28, 99, 133
Elliott, Roy/Alma 9, 37, 49, 61, 123, 129

Ellis, Havelock 89
Emerson, Ralph Waldo xiii, xxv, xxvi, 6, 49, 75–79, 81, 88, 130, 132

Farjeon, Eleanor 33
Faulkner, William xv
Fitzgerald, Gerald 131
Frost, Carol 38
Frost, Elinor xii, 38, 119
Frost, Isabel Moodie xi–xii, 35
Frost, Lesley xi–xiii, xix, 2, 115, 120
Frost, Marjorie 38
Frost, Robert Lee

IDEAS, ATTITUDES, STRATEGIES

Agnostic/spiritual drifter xvii, xx–xxii, 10, 79
Annunciation 31, 86, 88, 99
Barriers xviii, xxii, 24, 81, 93
Belief/believing xvi–xviii, xx–xxiii, 5, 9–11, 14, 23, 45, 50, 68, 82, 106–07, 127
Clarification/clarity/clear xvi–xvii, xix, xx, xxiii–xxiv, xxvi, 20, 64, 73, 79, 82, 118, 123
Contours xix–xx
Conversion xvi, xviii, 43–44, 46, 107, 122–23

144

Correspondence 17, 19, 30, 73, 77, 80, 83, 93

Dark/light xvi, xix, xx, xxiii–iv, 8, 15, 18–19, 20, 23, 39, 53, 58, 70, 77–78, 80, 82, 103, 118, 120–21

Design xix, xxiii, xxv, 14, 53, 62, 68, 71, 115, 122, 123, 130

Favor/grace/mercy 9, 25, 27–32, 35, 37–38, 41–47, 68, 93–94, 98–99, 129

Form xix, xxiii, xxv, 52–54, 61, 62, 67

Freethinker/free will/freedom 52, 65, 74, 105, 115, 117

Genesis/Garden of Eden/Adam and Eve 3–6, 54, 56, 58–59, 64, 121, 123

God Question xviii, xxii

✓Imagery/afterimagery xx, 1–3, 11–12, 122

Life after death 126–27

Loss 101–04, 107–09, 111–13

Metaphor/"as-if" xvi, xviii–xix, xxii–xxiii, xxvi, 5, 10, 11–12, 17, 43, 63, 68, 73–74, 79, 83, 91–92, 95, 101, 107, 110, 113, 120–21

Momentary stay against confusion xvii, xix, xxiii, 63

Mysticism 8, 32, 35, 77, 115

Order xvii, 58, 62, 70, 83

Reserve 6, 12, 14–20, 22, 45, 128–29

Revelation xxvi, 14, 19, 72, 73, 76, 78–79, 80–83, 85, 92, 95–96

Risk xxiii, 64–67, 117, 123

Salvation/saving/storing/keeping xii, xvii–xviii, 9, 43, 45–46, 61–62, 67, 101, 105–07, 109, 110, 113

✓Science 4–5, 11–12, 21, 64–66, 82, 85

Seeing/looking/watching 19, 23, 68, 93, 118–19, 122

Space xvi, 12, 64, 85

✓Synecdoche xix, xxiii, 1, 11, 54, 62, 64, 66, 68, 81, 83–85, 94

Time/life 56–58, 104, 117, 120

Trial by existence/earth as trial ground 53, 64, 68, 114, 115–16, 121–22

Types/typology xxvi, 75–76, 78, 130

Visitation 92, 95

Waste xxv, 88, 101–04

Wholeness/holiness xxiii, 34, 53, 60, 64, 66–68, 100, 106–07, 110, 113

WORKS CITED— BOOKS OF POETRY

A Boy's Will (1915) 14, 102, 108

North of Boston (1915) xvi, 118

New Hampshire (1923) 27–28, 30–31, 98

West-Running Brook (1928) 108

A Witness Tree (1942) 120

Complete Poems (1949) 64, 123

In the Clearing (1962) xix, 64, 103, 104, 118, 120

WORKS CITED—POEMS

Acceptance 121

Accidentally on Purpose xii, 62

Acquainted with the Night xvi

After Apple-Picking 2–6, 11, 59, 62

All Revelation xix, xxvi, 17, 18, 23, 72, 73, 74, 78, 80–84, 85, 93, 94

Away! xiii, 103, 121

A-Wishing Well 2

Ax-Helve, The 104

Bear, The xi, 133

Beech xx, 119–20

Birches 84, 110
Blue Ribbon at Amesbury, A xxii
Bond and Free 83–84
Boundless Moment, A 27, 31
Build Soil 85
Cabin in the Clearing, A xvi, xxiii–xxiv, 118, 122
Canis Major 119, 127
Census-Taker, The 109
Choose Something Like a Star 18–19, 63, 127
Come In 119
Death of the Hired Man, The 27, 30, 52, 108
Desert Places xx, 85, 108
Design xx, 53, 69–71
Directive xi, xii, xiii, xvii, 29, 62, 100, 102, 107–13, 118, 130, 131, 133
Draft Horse, The xx, 108, 121–22
Drumlin Woodchuck, A xxii, 9
Dust of Snow 29–30, 37–38, 61, 81, 128
Ends 101
Evening in a Sugar Orchard 63
Fear of Man, The 16
Fireflies in the Garden 63
For Once, Then, Something 24, 83, 85, 119
[Forgive, O Lord . . .] xii, 47
Generations of Men, The 109
Ghost House 102
Gift Outright, The 106–07, 120
Good-by and Keep Cold 15, 58
Grindstone, The 54–59, 104, 130
Hillside Thaw, A 7
How Hard It Is to Keep from Being King When It's in You and in the Situation 74
I Could Give All to Time xiii, 104–05

I Will Sing You One-O 96–99, 119
Impulse, The 101
[In Winter in the Woods Alone] xix, 120–21
Into My Own xvi, xix, 108, 120, 123
Iris by Night 26, 27, 32–35
Kitty Hawk xxi, xxiii, xxiv, 60, 64, 65, 66, 67, 68, 107, 108, 117
Last Mowing, The 120
Late Walk, A 102
Lesson for Today, The xvi, xxv, 53, 85, 108
Looking for a Sunset Bird in Winter 30–32
Masque of Mercy, A xvii–xviii, 21–22, 30, 36, 37, 38, 40, 42–46, 48, 49, 51, 58, 77–78, 82, 105–06, 107, 122
Masque of Reason, A xii–xiii, 4–5, 21, 24, 29, 38, 40, 42, 82, 107, 116–17, 122
Master Speed, The 15, 88
Meeting and Passing xii
Missive Missile, A 74
Most of It, The 92, 94–96
Mountain, The 111
Mowing 54
My Butterfly 102, 108
My November Guest 102
Need of Being Versed in Country Things, The 109, 132
Neither Out Far Nor In Deep 119
New Hampshire xxiii, 28, 63, 84
Night Light, The 108
Noche Triste, La xii
Not All There xii
Not to Keep 32
November 101, 102, 103, 105
Objection to Being Stepped On, The 57
October 102

Old Man's Winter Night, An 108
On Making Certain Anything Has Happened 118–19
Once by the Pacific 108
One More Brevity 19–24, 75, 92, 127, 128
"Out, Out—" 8
Parting 127
Passing Glimpse, A 24–25
Pasture, The xvi, 111, 118
Peaceful Shepherd, The 68
Pertinax 61
Pod of the Milkweed xxv, 101–02, 103–04
Prayer in Spring, A xii, 7, 14–15, 62, 94, 102–03, 127, 130
Provide, Provide xxii, 108, 134
Putting in the Seed 7
Quandary xxv
Question, A 83
Questioning Faces 24, 28–29, 30
Reluctance 102
Revelation xii, xix, 10, 17–18, 19, 73, 74, 80
Roadside Stand, A 37
Sand Dunes 105
Secret Sits, The xxvi, 12
Sitting by a Bush in Broad Sunlight 24
Soldier, A 32
Spring Pools 7–8, 85
Star in a Stone-Boat, A 23, 27, 79, 85
Star-Splitter, The 84
Stars xx, 119
Steeple on the House, A xii
Stopping by Woods on a Snowy Evening 27, 28, 121
Strong Are Saying Nothing, The 23, 122, 128, 134
Subverted Flower, The 7

Sycamore 120
Telephone, The xii
Time Out 78–79
Times Table, The 108
To Earthward xvi
To E. T. 32
[To prayer I think I go . . .] 38–39
Too Anxious for Rivers 4, 117–18
Tree at My Window 27
Trial by Existence, The xiii, 114, 115–16, 118
Two Look at Two 24, 27, 32, 92, 93–94, 95–96, 132
Two Tramps in Mud Time xiii, 67, 104
Unharvested 59
Vanishing Red, The 8
Voice Ways 119
Waiting 102
West-Running Brook xx, xxi, xxiv–xxv, 13, 15, 51, 57, 78, 86, 87–92, 101, 102, 105, 132
Wind and the Rain, The 102, 103
Wood-Pile, The 59

WORKS CITED—PROSE

Amherst Student, The, Letter to xxv, 51, 52–53, 55, 61, 62
"Constant Symbol, The" xviii, 5, 67, 77, 104
"Education by Poetry" xviii, 11–12, 62, 63, 82, 133
"Figure a Poem Makes, The" xvi, xxvi, 63, 73
King Jasper, Introduction to 16–17, 73, 132
"Metaphors" 89
"Poet's Next of Kin in a College, The" 68

"Prerequisites, The" xix
Private Notebook 39–41, 129
"Sermon" 50–51

Greenleaf, Robert K. xi

Harris, Mark 8–9, 132, 133
Hemingway, Ernest xv, xxiii–xxiv
Heraclitus 89

Isaacs, Elizabeth xi

James, William xiii, 52, 62, 75, 82, 96

Landor, Walter Savage 2
Lathem, Edward Connery 125, 126, 127, 132
Lowance, Mason I. Jr. 131–32
Lucretius xxv, 89, 118
Lynen, John F. 55

MacGillivray, Father Arthur 64, 127–28
Miller, Perry 76
Morrison, Theodore 10, 27, 110, 130–31, 133
Munson, Gorham B. 126, 131

Nitchie, George W. xvii, 103, 126, 131

O'Donnell, William G. 125

Pack, Robert 121–22
Pearson, Norman Holmes 130

Puritans/Puritanism xvi, xxvi, 75–76, 107

Reichert, Rabbi Victor xi, 41, 50–51, 125, 126
Rodman, Selden xi, 122

Sartre, Jean-Paul xx, xxiv, 71
Sergeant, Elizabeth Shepley xi, 35, 83, 109, 116, 123
Smythe, Daniel 129
Stanlis, Peter J. xvii
Stevens, Wallace xxii
Swedenborg/Swedenborgianism xi, xii, xiii, 8, 35, 75, 77

Tate, Allan 122
Taylor, Edward 76
Tharpe, Jac 125
Thomas, Edward 32–34
Thomism xviii
Thompson, Lawrance xviii, xxi, 9, 35, 39, 46, 49–50, 51, 53, 64, 68, 75, 89, 115, 119, 127, 129, 130, 132
Transcendentalism xxii, 77, 79, 130
Trilling, Lionel xvi

Unitarianism xvii–xviii
Untermeyer, Louis 9, 32, 38–39, 79, 104

Waggoner, Hyatt Howe xx–xxi
Whicher, George 33
Whitman, Walt 71
Winters, Yvor xvii, xx, xxi

Yeats, William Butler 68, 95, 113, 131